The Making of a Mediator

Michael D. Lang
Alison Taylor

The Making of a Mediator

Mediator

Developing Artistry in Practice

JOSSEY-BASS
A Wiley Company
San Francisco

Published by Jossey-Bass
A Wiley Imprint
989 Market Street, San Francisco, CA 94103-1741   www.josseybass.com

Jossey-Bass books and products are available through most bookstores. To
contact Jossey-Bass directly call our Customer Care Department within the U.S.
at (800) 956-7739, outside the U.S. at (317) 572-3986 or fax (317) 572-4002.

Jossey-Bass also publishes its books in a variety of electronic formats. Some
content that appears in print may not be available in electronic books.

Library of Congress Cataloging-in-Publication Data

Lang, Michael D., date.
   The making of a mediator : developing artistry in practice / Michael
D. Lang and Alison Taylor. — 1st ed.
     p.   cm.
   Includes bibliographical references and index.
   ISBN 0-7879-4992-2
   1. Conflict management. 2. Mediation. I. Taylor, Alison, date.
II. Title.
HD42 L.36 2000
658.4'053—dc21   99-050521

FIRST EDITION
HB Printing   10 9 8 7 6 5 4

Contents

"Facts which at first seem improbable will, even on scant explanation, drop the cloak which has hidden them and stand forth in naked and simple beauty."

Galileo

"The sage never tries to store things up.
The more he does for others, the more he has.
The more he gives to others, the greater his abundance.
The Tao of heaven is pointed but does no harm.
The Tao of the sage is work without effort."

Lao Tsu

Preface

Artistry is not a destination, a place where mediators can settle comfortably, secure in the knowledge that they have attained the highest level of professional competence. Rather, artistry is a journey, a process of exploring and testing the range and application of professional knowledge and skills. At times the journey is uncomfortable, such as when mediators experience the obstacles and challenges to excellence, when they bump up against the limits of their knowledge or skill, or when they fail. Other times the journey is sublime, such as when they experience the exhilaration of matching their skills and knowledge to the needs of disputants, when their work seems effortless, flowing, and intuitive. Above all, artistry is a mind-set—a commitment to curiosity and exploration, to excellence and learning.

When we started on our paths as mediators about twenty years ago, the field was in its early years and the questions about the nature and form of mediation practice with which we struggled then were basic. We were asking, How do we define mediation? What are the elements of the mediation process? What are the steps, stages, or phases of a mediation? How do people learn to be mediators? Although the field continues to grapple with these questions, new and more intricate issues have emerged.

Practitioners, researchers, and scholars debate the implications of facilitative and evaluative forms of practice, and vigorous dialogue has ensued over problem-solving and transformative approaches to mediation. The certification, or credentialing, of mediators has become a key issue for practitioners in many locales. Practice in a broad range of new contexts and arenas has evolved along with novel forms of intervention. Each area of practice has developed wonderful voices describing essential knowledge and skills and prescribing appropriate methods. Researchers, scholars, and practitioners have contributed to a large and valuable body of literature.

What, then, in this proliferation of ideas, models, and theories, unifies mediators? What can help them hold onto the essential aspects of mediation when each practitioner and each context represents differences in form, methods, strategies, and goals? To advance the field of mediation practice, mediators need to examine their assumptions and question their beliefs and practices in ways that help them make clear, thoughtful, and perhaps difficult choices about what is essential, what should be discarded, and what requires further investigation.

Unless mediators understand the underlying theoretical principles that influence and shape their practices, they are merely talented mechanics trying out one tool after another without understanding why a particular tool might be useful and what results are likely to flow. They are skilled mimics who apply techniques and interventions without fully considering the reasons behind the approaches, without understanding the likely consequences, without the ability to evaluate the success or failure of those interventions, and without the tools and resources to learn from each experience. When this occurs, mediators may be capable and frequently effective, but they will never achieve artistry, the highest level of skill to which they can aspire. Some assert, as one participant in a workshop did, that there is nothing wrong with mediocrity, that "good enough" is acceptable. Mediators need to hold out for something beyond mediocrity. They need to aspire to attain a level of competence, resourcefulness, and effectiveness that we have called *artistry*.

Our intent in this book is to broaden and deepen the thinking in the field by asking questions about the nature of competency in mediation practice. This book presents the principles that support the development of artistry and describes methods and practices that lead to excellence in professional practice. The book's three major areas of focus—artistry, reflection, and interactive process— are synergistic. They need one another in order to develop. By thinking about them in the ways we present, you will change the way you think about your work, with the inevitable consequence that you will change your way of working. This will be true no matter what type of dispute you work on or at what level.

We want to change mediation practice by changing not what you think (the form or approach you use) but how you think about your practice. We begin by asserting that our approach to the development of excellence in mediation—artistry—is not limited to any one form of practice. We offer universally applicable methods and principles. We next ask you to make explicit that which is often implicit. By making your theories, beliefs, information, ideas, and knowledge more accessible, you will be better able to understand the choices you make as mediators. By developing the habits and methods of reflective practice, you will learn to make use of the experiences you have in your practice to improve the quality, relevance, and impact of your interventions. Through attention to and use of critical moments in mediation, you will learn to be intentional and focused in your practice. The ultimate outcome we seek is that by understanding your unique set of theories and their application to your practice, you will ultimately make more internally consistent and therefore more effective choices during the mediation process.

This book presents not an esoteric discussion of purely theoretical principles but a practical and necessary set of methods and approaches that will move you forward in your development as a mediator. The results of adopting the methods and principles in this book will be direct and positive consequences for your work with clients. In this age when mediators are increasingly held accountable for their services as dispute resolvers (whether in government agencies, courts, or community settings, or as privately paid mediators), the concepts we describe have a very pragmatic application. By being mindful in your approach and by solidly connecting your practice to your theories, you will start to practice more consistently and with greater focus and efficacy. You will find increased satisfaction in your practice, your mediations will reflect your competence and flexibility, and the disputants will have a constructive and highly effective experience.

Once you have identified and seen the effect of the beliefs, principles, and values that shape your practice, you will be able to make choices about retaining, replacing, or discarding these theories. By going through the processes outlined in this book, you will be able to retain the best of what your learning and experience have taught you, as well as to modify or replace those elements that seem inconsistent or unworkable. Creation is brought about by the interplay of conscious intent and receptive openness. Awareness of the principles that inform your practice, together with a beginner's mind—open and receptive—will enhance your creative potential.

It has been said that the unexamined life is not worth living. We are inviting you to look through a new lens, to examine your assumptions and habits in order to make your actions more purposeful and effective. Exploring this terrain is a necessary first step in a journey that leads toward professional competence, and ultimately to artistry. This book is a guidebook as well as an invitation to walk that path.

We believe in the potential of each person who reads this book to experience artistry. Artistry is egalitarian, not elitist; it is available to everyone. There are many paths toward artistry. Whether and how artistry appears in your practice will be determined by whether you have the necessary core skills and knowledge and are able to use the methods and principles of reflective practice and interactive process. For each reader of this book, the path will be unique. At the same time, there are principles, methods, practices, habits, and skills that are useful to all of us on our journey.

As teachers, coaches, and trainers, we are deeply committed to helping mediators develop the habits and practices we describe in this book. We have great hope for our field; at the same time we are deeply concerned with the failure of mediators to continue to seek their potential. We believe in the potential of mediators to develop their knowledge and skills in ways that are personally fulfilling, professionally honorable, and worthy of great esteem.

Although this book embodies theories, practices, methods, principles, exercises, and ideas that we believe are vital to the future of our field, what has driven us to complete the book is our belief in our and your potential to be excellent, to deliver high-quality, competent, and resourceful services. At its core, the book is about the aspiration to achieve that potential.

How the Book Is Organized

This book addresses both a theoretical framework and a pragmatic approach to practice in order to provide both conceptual understanding and a practical methodology. We are practitioners who are deeply concerned with the applied aspects of theoretical material. We want to understand how theory can and does shape practice. We are also educators and trainers and we have a passionate commitment to exploring and understanding how our methods of practice reflect our beliefs and values. The connection between theory and practice, as tested and analyzed through research, is central to our inquiry into professional excellence, or artistry. This book describes the key conceptual notions that are the guideposts on the path toward excellence in practice, as well as the methods and skills that are the tools needed to make the journey.

As mediators and educators, we use questions to elicit ideas and awareness, to shape conversations, to encourage exploration, and to inspire discovery. We therefore begin by identifying many of the questions we asked ourselves as we developed our ideas for this book. We wondered, How do mediators learn to be effective at dealing with disputes? We wanted to understand not so much the criteria by which excellence might be measured, but rather the learning process that elevates professional practice toward competence and effectiveness. Although we have an interest in the content of curricula, we are mostly concerned with the process by which novice mediators learn to employ the knowledge and skills of a mediator, advancing through the stages of professional development to become competent and resourceful practitioners. We want to understand the path that mediators follow on their journey from novice to artist.

To begin answering this question, we created a model of professional development (see Chapter One) that describes movement along a spiral path, a continuum that begins with the *novice* and passes through the stages of *apprentice* and *practitioner* to artist. The model both explains the path of professional development and describes the learning tasks at each stage. The elements of this model will be familiar to those who have studied adult education. We do not claim that the basic principles are original; in fact, we know of other compatible models. However, we believe that our model contains important elements that we originated, and we believe that our application of the model is unique.

Having begun to explore the process of professional development, we next asked ourselves, What is this mysterious, transcendent, and some would say ineffable quality we have designated as artistry? What is the object of our aspiration?

In considering the nature of artistry, we wanted to identify hallmarks, behaviors that could be noted and identified, that would signal that artistry is present. Recognizing that artistry appears in different forms and guises, we sought concrete, observable phenomena that might mark the presence of artistry. Our exploration led us to identify the hallmarks presented in Chapter Two.

As pragmatists, we next asked ourselves, What practical steps will help a mediator achieve artistry? We wanted to understand what tools are necessary to make the journey. To achieve artistry requires knowledge, an understanding of the principles that support professional practice, an awareness of the traditions, beliefs, and mind-sets that characterize mediation. In addition, the mediator aspiring toward artistry must be skilled, must have the ability to manipulate a variety of practice techniques, and must be able to apply those techniques strategically. These elements—knowledge and skill—are fundamental.

Artistry represents an expression of excellence, a commitment to curiosity, learning, and exploration. Yet we have a growing concern that practitioners in the developing profession of mediation are not being encouraged to be curious, to be learners and explorers. We have a sense that mediators, and the field in general, are not achieving their potential. There is a lack of effort to assist mediators systematically and methodically to move from that early stage of professional development (what we have called the novice) to the role of accomplished, effective, and resourceful mediator (the artist). Training programs teach the novice a range of practice tools and their application. Novices do not, however, learn the conceptual grounding necessary for effective and competent practice. Without the ability to understand the reasoning behind intervention strategies and techniques, mediators invariably construct rigid and inflexible categories for characterizing disputes that frame issues narrowly, based on a set of prescribed problem sets. These mediators then apply skills without an understanding of how to assess whether their analysis of the problem is accurate, whether the application of the technique is suited to the situation, and whether the intervention is having its desired effect. The result may be adequate practice but it lacks the potential for artistry. Artistry requires more than an ability to apply techniques skillfully; it also requires a grounding in theory, the discipline of reflective practice, and the purposeful application of interactive process.

We have organized the book into three parts. In Part One we respond to a number of questions about artistry—its importance in professional practice, its nature and sources, and the hallmarks that evidence its presence in practice. We also consider whether artistry can be learned, and the methods by which instructors and coaches can help practitioners develop the discipline and mind-set that lead to artistry. In Chapter One, we provide a context for understanding the path that leads from novice to artist by presenting our dynamic four-stage model of professional development and by discussing the methods, principles, and practices that assist mediators along that path. We also discuss the relationship of artistry to intuition. In Chapter Two we present the hallmarks of artistry, the characteristics that identify artistic practice. Chapter Three concludes the section with examples that illustrate the methods by which practitioners can be taught to develop the habits, skills, and mind-set that will help them advance along the path of professional development toward artistry.

The chapters in Part Two present our beliefs about reflective practice and the methods that lead to competent practice. To engage in reflective practice, mediators must first identify their working assumptions—the beliefs, values, and habits that shape their practices. In Chapter Four we explain the nature and function of formulation—the effort to construct meaning out of experiences, events, and interactions. We consider not only the process by which formulations arise but also why they are vital to effective mediation practice. We present methods for making explicit what is essentially tacit. Becoming aware of these assumptions allows mediators to be intentional in their professional work.

Chapter Five introduces the concept of a constellation of theories, the idea that everyone has a number of principles that function as lenses through which they view and make sense of their experiences. Mediators have and use theories, though generally randomly and not purposefully. By becoming aware of the constellation of theories on which their intervention decisions are made, mediators can become deliberate and resourceful, using their theories intentionally to guide their application of strategies and techniques.

The principles, practices, and mind-set of the reflective practitioner are described in Chapter Six. Developing the habits of reflection, both while engaged in practice and subsequently, and being able to form working hypotheses and test them through a process of experimentation are hallmarks of the reflective practitioner. We also explain the methods for and goals of reflective practice. Finally, we explore how reflective practice opens the mediator's range of options, and present methods that develop artistry in mediation.

The chapters in Part Three illustrate that implementing a reflective approach requires awareness of the patterns of interaction that arise and extend throughout the mediation. In Chapter Seven we present the concept of critical moments, or choice points, during mediation. To develop artistry in practice, mediators must be able to sense when during the events and circumstances of the mediation the parties are at a juncture that invites the mediator to intervene in order to implement some strategy or technique. Critical moments present challenges and opportunities that require the mediator to make decisions that will affect the subsequent path of the mediation process.

Chapter Eight looks at interactive process. Each action of a participant or the mediator influences the behavior, attitude, and responses of the other participants. We want mediators to become aware and to make effective use of the aspects of interactive process to reflect on their strategies and interventions and to make choices while understanding the potential impact of those choices on others.

Finally, in Chapter Nine, we consider flow, the sense of moving effortlessly with clients. Flow is a state of being, an experience that cannot be created, but mediators can enhance the likelihood of achieving this state by attending to those behaviors that support or block flow. Artistry is reflected in the experience of flow.

Finally, in the concluding chapter we draw together the theories and practices described throughout the book and present ideas for their application in mediation training programs, in courses of graduate study, in coaching and supervision, and in the development of methods and criteria for assessing mediator competency.

We invite you to explore this book. We have organized it in a way that mirrors our approach to teaching the principles and practices we present. We are not prescriptive teachers, so we will not insist that you read each chapter in order. In our teaching, and in this book, we acknowledge that each learner is unique and will proceed along her own path. We have provided a number of exercises and other materials that will assist your exploration of artistry. We recognize that the journey from novice to artist is distinctly individual. We invite you to follow the path toward artistry—to take your own journey.

Acknowledgments

We want to acknowledge the many contributors and supporters who have helped us on our way from concept to manuscript. Although we are duly proud of the ideas and methods we have developed, we acknowledge that we stand on the shoulders of many scholars, researchers, and practitioners whose work has stimulated, supported, guided, and advanced our work—particularly the seminal work of Donald Schön, whose books have inspired, informed, and at times perplexed us.

The methods we have developed, particularly the elicitive coaching model, grew out of extensive experience in supervising interns, training mediators, and coaching practitioners. Examples from these sessions fill the book. Without the opportunity to learn with and from our students, these ideas would be little more than our own untested musings.

Many friends and colleagues also contributed to the book through their review of portions of the manuscript, in extensive conversations over coffee at professional meetings, and as co-trainers. Listing all of them would require a separate chapter. We hope they will find suitable acknowledgment and appreciation in these few words. We specifically want to acknowledge five colleagues who read and commented on the final version of the manuscript: Lynn Jacob, James Melamed, Sylvia McMechan, Richard McGuigan, and Robert Benjamin.

Books are the aspirations of authors brought to life by their editor, who patiently nurtures the authors' ideas into a publishable form. In that regard, we are deeply indebted to Leslie Berriman for her critical reading and nurturing presence.

Finally, and most important, as two busy practitioner-teachers we could not have even considered the idea of writing this book without the patience, support, advice, and assistance of our families. To them we offer our appreciation and our love.

February 2000   Michael D. Lang
Pittsburgh, Pennsylvania
Alison Taylor
Hillsboro, Oregon

The Authors

Michael D. Lang is professor and special adviser for program and faculty development in the Masters in Conflict Analysis and Management Program at Royal Roads University in Victoria, British Columbia. He is on the faculty of Woodbury College in Montpelier, Vermont, and was founding director of the Individualized Master of Arts Program in Conflict Resolution at Antioch University in Yellow Spring, Ohio. Lang is a graduate of Harvard College and Boston University School of Law.

Lang has been a mediator, trainer, and consultant for over twenty years. As a private practitioner he has mediated family, business, organization, and public policy disputes. As a consultant and trainer in conflict resolution, he has worked with universities, business organizations, religious congregations, and nonprofit groups.

As a trainer, Lang has presented seminars, both introductory and advanced, for family courts, mediation centers, and professional associations. He has presented seminars and workshops at professional meetings in the United States and Canada and has been a visiting faculty member at Hamline Law School Dispute Resolution Institute, the Justice Institute of British Columbia, Duquesne University, and Carleton University.

Active in many professional activities, Lang has served on the boards of directors and as an officer of local, regional, state, and national professional organizations in the field of conflict resolution. He is a former president and member of the board of directors of the Academy of Family Mediators.

Lang has served as editor-in-chief of *Mediation Quarterly* since 1995, and he edits "Resolution" and "MIRC News," which can be found at the website www.mediate.com.

Alison Taylor is a licensed professional counselor and has been a professional mediator for over twenty years in public and private mediation. She is coauthor of the now-classic text, *Mediation: A Comprehensive Guide to Resolving Conflicts Without Litigation*, published by Jossey-Bass in 1984. She has published articles in *Mediation Quarterly* and *The Association of Family Conciliation Courts Review*, and is on the editorial board of *Mediation Quarterly*.

Taylor and Lang worked together to refine the practice of reflective supervision at Antioch University's Master's Program in Conflict Resolution, where Taylor served as a faculty adviser and guest lecturer. She currently teaches mediation skills and conflict theory at Portland State University's Master's in Conflict Resolution program and its School of Extended Studies, as well as courses at Marylhurst University.

For over ten years, Taylor was the training coordinator at a county divorce mediation service; she is currently employed as a trainer and supervisor of interns. She is designing and implementing peer, family, and victim-offender mediation services for Inter-Change, a county therapeutic community treatment center for substance-abusing offenders. Taylor provides teaching and consultation in her private practice. She is a member of the Academy of Family Mediators and of the Oregon Mediation Association.

The Making of a Mediator

Part One

Artistry

Chapter One

Developing Artistry

The mediation process is proceeding well. You are tracking the discussion, focused on the overarching issues as well as the moment-to-moment exchange of perspectives. You have a heightened awareness of your own place in the process and are mindful of the parties, the issues, and their interactions. Your attention is so intense that you are unaware of time passing. The conversation and your interventions are effortless, yet measured and purposeful. There is a sense of progress, without an effort to make something happen. You are engaged, pulled into the tasks of the mediation, but the work seems effortless and graceful. The process is elegant, flowing, and productive.

This is the experience of *artistry* in mediation practice. At some time in your practice (or in other endeavors) you have experienced this sense of *flow*, of operating in a way that seemed automatic yet being fully aware of and responsive to the shifting interactions among you and the disputing parties. You have had the experience of being calm, focused, fully engaged, and effective. It is a powerful experience. Moreover, the clients experienced the flow as well and benefited from your ability to work gracefully and effortlessly with them.

This book presents the process and methods that lead mediators to artistry, and describes the journey from beginning student to accomplished professional, from novice to artist. We use the metaphor of a journey throughout this book because artistry is not a product, produced by the application and practice of a discrete set of skills and techniques. Artistry is an ongoing process of reflection, learning, understanding, and exploration. In this book we show you both the complexity and the simplicity of artistry as applied to mediation practice, in the hope that you will aspire to artistry in your own practice. We want you to extend the journey of your professional development, advancing your knowledge and skills, enriching your experience, and using the principles and methods of reflective practice and interactive process to seek and attain artistry.

Artistry may seem an ineffable quality: intangible, idiosyncratic, and difficult to capture in words. But the experience of artistry in professional practice is genuine, meaningful, and substantial. Skeptics frequently assert that artistry is like a blinding flash of light—a moment of brilliance that occurs by chance and is not replicable. Its presence can be acknowledged but not understood. We believe that artistry can be defined in terms of behaviors, attributes, and practices—what we have called *hallmarks of artistry*. Once artistry has been defined in terms of observable, identifiable operations, mediators can learn to develop the habits and practices that lead to it.

In addition to having experienced the flow that characterizes artistry, you have also experienced the products of artistic practice, often in the ordinary events of your lives. Artistry in any endeavor is not just the best expression of that endeavor. It is also the manifestation of a person using all his or her knowledge and skill in such a way that others notice the difference not only in the product but also in the process by which the product is accomplished. Many of you are amateur photographers. Your camera uses the same photographic and optic principles as those used by professional photographers and you use a similar type of film. Some of your photographs are quite ordinary; they capture the subject, they are in focus, and they provide a lasting memory of a moment or a scene. Yet in a roll of twenty-four photographs, perhaps one or two, if you are fortunate, are noticeably different and seem to have an indescribable element that distinguishes them from the others. What makes these images possible is that the photographer's process (what some may refer to as her "eye") has merged into the outcome, giving the photograph a quality of excellence that other people in addition to the photographer can identify and acknowledge.

The Qualities of Artistry

The difficulty with using a term such as *artistry* is that it may connote something less capable of being defined and measured and therefore less rigorous than scientific knowledge. Donald Schön, whose work on reflective practice has provided inspiration and substance for our thinking, has noted that "outstanding practitioners are not said to have more professional knowledge but more 'wisdom,' 'talent,' 'intuition,' or 'artistry'—They are used as junk categories, attaching names to phenomena that elude conventional strategies of explanation" (Schön, 1987, p. 13). Those who use such terms as *intuition, talent,* and *wisdom* dismiss artistry as lacking a substantive quality because they lack the analytical tools to appreciate and understand its elements and its application to professional practice. Some may reject artistry as less measurable, and thus less important, than phenomena such as scientific and scholarly knowledge. In contrast, we believe that artistry is a definable, observable, and determinable quality that can be subject to the rigors of analysis. Thus professionals can learn to recognize, identify, understand, and practice artistry. It is characterized by wisdom, talent, and intuition, and people can learn to apply these elements in their endeavors, with intention and diligence, so that artistry is not merely a fortuitous convergence of a number of personal talents and abilities but arises purposefully (Goleman, Kaufman, and Ray, 1993).

To assist our students in understanding the attributes, qualities, substance, and elements of artistry, we often ask them to complete an activity: to think of a moment in their professional practice when they experienced something quite unusual, an ability to perform in ways they could not define—in short, a successful flow experience. (Please see Chapter Nine for an in-depth discussion of the nature of flow and its place in the development of artistry.) We then use their answers to illustrate that artistry is grounded in the competent exercise of practice skills, in a thorough understanding of the foundational principles of the profession, and in extensive, relevant experience.

The following example, taken from one of our mediation courses, dramatically illustrates the three-part foundation for the development of artistry. When we asked volunteers to present their success stories, a student responded by telling about her role as a social worker assisting children who had been removed from their parents' care because of parental neglect or abuse. A year after a group of children had been placed in foster care, the social worker convened a meeting that was attended by the foster parents, the biological mother, and the children. The purpose of the meeting was to consider the possibility of the children being returned to their mother. During the meeting the student asked the children to talk with their mother, to tell her what they liked and missed most about her as their mom. The children spoke lovingly about and to their mother. As a result of the meeting, and particularly because of the conversation between the children and their mother, everyone committed to working toward reuniting the children and their mother. When we asked the student how she came to the decision to convene the meeting, she replied, "It just seemed like a good idea." When we asked about her decision to invite the children to speak to their mother, the student replied, "The idea just came to me; it wasn't something I had planned."

At the time of these interactions, the student was unable to analyze or explain her decision-making process; in fact, she felt that something outside her awareness had guided her decisions—an influence that she identified as "intuition." Curiously, she wanted to dismiss the significance of her decisions by claiming that they had occurred outside her awareness, that they were not within her control, and that they were not the product of a rational, logical, analytical process. If they were not susceptible to scientific inquiry, they had no substance and therefore no validity. Those of us listening to her story, however, recognized artistry. The social worker had read the signals of the participants in the meeting, brought her knowledge and experience to bear, and created a flow experience, a moment of artistry.

We asked the social worker to reflect on that meeting and assisted her in deconstructing the events in order to demonstrate that what seemed to be intuition was in fact a series of decisions grounded in her knowledge, skill, and expertise and shaped by her attention to and understanding of the interaction among the participants. We asked her to identify the areas of knowledge (both theory and practice skills) she had acquired as a social worker. She responded that she had earned a bachelor's degree in social work that included courses on family systems and family dynamics, and that she had learned about the developmental needs of children, read materials on the impact on children of separation and loss, and participated in a number of relevant in-service training courses. When asked about her experience, she told us that she had been a social worker for more than fifteen years, that she had dealt with hundreds of families, and that many of her cases had involved abused and neglected children. Additionally, as the mother of two she had personal knowledge of children and family life.

As we painstakingly moved through this inquiry, a process that lasted nearly forty-five minutes, she became aware that her decisions in the meeting had been the product of her education and training and her knowledge and skills, polished and refined by years of experience. What she referred to as intuition was in fact a highly developed capacity to synthesize theory and technique into decisions and actions that were responsive, competent, and effective. Underlying her decision making was a rigorous and analytical process grounded in competent practice, groomed by years of experience, and guided by a grasp of theoretical principles. Artistry does not come out of a vacuum but appears when knowledge and skill converge with sensitivity to interactive experiences.

The social worker's decisions occurred so rapidly that they appeared to be intuitive. Yet as Mihaly Csikszentmihalyi (1996, p. 1), in his study of creativity, has noted, "a genuinely creative accomplishment is almost never the result of a sudden insight, a light bulb flashing on in the dark, but comes after years of hard work." Responding to our questions about her education, training, and experience, the student gradually became aware that her creative approach to the problem facing this family was rooted in the foundation of her knowledge, skills, and experience, which she had applied with care and purpose to the interaction. Her decisions fused the best she had into a new approach, one that flowed out of the events of the moment and was responsive to the issues at hand.

Although the situation appeared similar to countless others she had experienced in her years as a social worker, it demonstrated particular competence. To the faculty and fellow students listening to her story, her resourcefulness and ingenuity were apparent. The power of her interventions was not measured simply by the results they had achieved but by the inventiveness, creativity, and artistry she had displayed. Csikszentmihalyi (1996, p. 27) also asserts, "We must foster intuition to anticipate changes before they occur; empathy to understand that which cannot be clearly expressed; wisdom to see the connection between apparently unrelated events; and creativity to discover new ways of defining problems, new rules that will make it possible to adapt to the unexpected."

Understanding the children's need to reclaim their mother; the mother's need to regain her self-image as a worthy, capable parent; and the foster parents' commitment to the children's welfare, the social worker found an approach that would artfully and elegantly address each person's concerns. This example demonstrates our basic points about artistry: it is grounded in knowledge and skill, it requires attention to the interactive circumstances, and it emerges when individuals bring their own interpretation to events and thus yield a new and elegant approach.

The Roots of Artistry

More than the mere accumulation of knowledge, skill, and experience, artistry is attained when professionals are sufficiently grounded in, skilled at, and knowledgeable about the key components of their professions or activities that they can bring their own unique perspective and interpretation to bear on the practice. According to Schön (1987, p. 13), "Artistry is an exercise of intelligence, a kind of knowing, though different in crucial respects from our standard model of professional knowledge. It is not inherently mysterious; it is rigorous in its own terms; and we can learn a great deal about it . . . by carefully studying the performance of unusually competent performers." Artistry begins with a strong foundation in the skills, techniques, and strategies as well as the theories of one's profession or endeavor. The artist must also have the ability to synthesize knowledge and skills in the moment of interaction, to integrate theory and technique into a series of strategies and interventions. Most professional schools provide instruction in the basic concepts and principles that underpin the profession, and offer opportunities for students to learn a repertoire of skills and methods for applying theory to problem situations. Whether in schools of art, medicine, social work, law, business, science, or education, students learn the fundamental elements of their profession. "A musician must learn the musical tradition, the notation system, the way instruments are played before she can think of writing a new song; before an inventor can improve an airplane design he has to learn physics, aerodynamics and why birds don't fall out of the sky" (Csikszentmihalyi, 1996, p. 8). Artistry emerges only after the professional is sufficiently educated in history, traditions, theory, principles, and practices.

Not all professionals are artists. Many may be competent, effective, knowledgeable, and accomplished; some may even occasionally display a brilliance that approaches artistry. However, artistry requires more than competence in the performance of the essential skills of professional practice, and more than the capacity to apply theory in a thoughtful and analytical manner. It is how a professional responds to the unique circumstances, the surprising events, that arise in professional practice that separates the artist from the practitioner.

For every professional the manifestation of artistry will be unique, reflecting the individual's innate abilities and talents, which have been enhanced through the acquisition of specialized knowledge and skills. In athletics, physical ability and talent, coaching, practice, and determination will not likely help a person become a professional. At the same time, talented individuals can benefit from coaching to develop ways of utilizing their innate abilities and to allow their artistic expression to emerge. Most people have some unique, inborn abilities that provide the basic foundation for achievement. With sufficient motivation and discipline, they can experience artistry.

Too many people attempt to mimic a practitioner they regard as an expert. Lacking the same training, experience, and abilities, they often fail to achieve the measure of artistry they so admire. In attempting to imitate the expert, practitioners may fall short of their goal. Experts are useful in demonstrating the potential of artistry. Mediators can learn by observing them, studying their techniques, and reading their books. As a result, mediators may become competent practitioners, but not artists.

In the mythic tales of the hero's journey and in the bildungsroman novels depicting the young person's travels to adulthood, the protagonist starts his journey as a beginner, one who is unschooled, unskilled, and curious. Through a series of events or trials, the beginner gains knowledge, experience, skill, and the ability to innovate when faced with surprising and unique circumstances. In mediation, the practitioner follows a similar path. She starts as a beginner, learning through doing and under the tutelage of a guide or teacher who provides feedback and helps her learn from her mistakes, building on her successes, and becoming competent. Yet most mediators want more than the ability to practice competently. They want the heightened experience of artistry. They want to experience the flow, the flashes of brilliance, and the sense of creative energy that characterize artistic practice.

Our premise in this book is that mediators can experience more inventive, fulfilling, and stimulating moments in their practices. They can flow without effort. We believe that it is through the use of the methods and principles of reflective practice and interactive process that mediators can generate and experience such moments.

To understand the path by which professionals travel toward artistry, we turn to the *dynamic model of professional development*. This four-part model depicts the developmental stages through which professionals advance on their journey from novice to artist.

Artistry as a Dynamic Process

Artistry develops over time and reflects a person's professional development. The dynamic four-stage model depicts this process of professional advancement (see Figure 1.1). Each quadrant of the model represents a collection of elements that together signify a stage in professional development. The division lines are artificial and the transition from one stage to the next is not necessarily identified by a distinctive set of markers. The division into stages, however, helps identify qualities and characteristics of the path to artistry. Through diligence, patience, and intention, along with the desire to proceed along the path, each professional can make the journey to artistry.

Stage One: The Novice

The path to artistry requires that each person begin at the place of the novice. Novices are uninformed about a subject, unaware of what they will need to learn, and uncertain about where they might obtain the skills and knowledge or how they can be applied. When you embark on a course of study to learn a profession, a musical

Figure 1.1. The Dynamic Four-Stage Model of Professional Development.

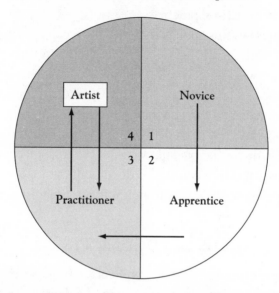

Novice: unaware, unskilled. *Apprentice:* somewhat aware, somewhat skilled. *Practitioner:* aware, skilled. *Artist:* heightened awareness, heightened skills.

instrument, or a sport, you have a *beginner's mind*—open, unassuming, available, not knowing what to expect, looking for information. Beginners have little knowledge of the subject, are unfamiliar with what they will need to know in order to gain proficiency, are unaware of the techniques they will be taught, and are uncertain of the process of their training.

The novice mediator is one who may not have observed or participated in a mediation, may not have read any books or articles about mediation, and may have little if any knowledge of the practice. This is a person who has had no previous mediation training, who knows neither what he will need to learn or the nature of the learning process. The novice is interested in learning and is excited about gaining the knowledge and skills of the mediator, understanding the nature of mediation practice, and experiencing the role of the mediator. Initial interest in mediation may have been sparked by conversations with colleagues or friends. Moreover, many of those who embark on training in mediation may have acted as a mediator informally or spontaneously, without the benefit of understanding an organized and systematic approach or without knowledge of practices and principles. To develop basic competency, mediators in this stage need models and examples as well as training and experience, accompanied by constructive feedback from coaches.

Stage Two: The Apprentice

The person in this stage of professional development has a working knowledge of some of the principles and skills of mediation. Having completed a basic mediation training program, the apprentice has participated in role-plays and case studies and as a result has developed a sense of how mediation works. The apprentice has addressed many questions of practice and understands that the knowledge he or she has already gained is merely a small portion of what there is to learn about mediation. Apprentices have limited skills, yet they have a feeling for the process and for the role of mediator. Apprentice mediators find joy in the opportunity to use what they have learned.

At the same time, however, apprentices lack experience in interaction, in putting their knowledge and skills into practice. They seek opportunities to test their knowledge and skills, are eager to be mediators, and seek to experience the satisfaction of the role. This is when apprentice mediators seek mentors to provide guidance and to help them obtain the practical experience needed to develop competence. Under the supervision and guidance of more experienced mediators, apprentices learn to apply the knowledge and skills gained in the basic training program to the practice of mediation. They maintain a thirst for knowledge and seek additional training to enlarge their repertoire of skills. Apprentices have gained a sense of what the practice requires, of its potential and its requirements.

Stage Three: The Practitioner

Skilled professionals operate at this stage most of the time. Their work is grounded in theory (knowledge) and they have a broad repertoire of practice skills. These practitioners bring their knowledge and skills together with sufficient experience to know when and how to employ their abilities in positive, constructive, and effective ways. Practitioner mediators are accomplished professionals, they are well regarded by their peers, and their services are valued by their clients. They are knowledgeable and have considerable experience in a variety of practice situations. They work with purpose and care. During interactive moments, practitioners are able to detect nuances, the subtle distinctions between situations that may appear similar on the surface but require a unique response.

Practitioners continue to seek knowledge and skills and may participate in advanced training programs, although they view themselves as proficient, skillful, and talented. They are generally interested in new concepts and techniques, and often invent them. Practitioners are also trainers for novices and mentors to apprentices. They view themselves as capable and able to impart to others the wisdom, knowledge, and skills they have acquired through years of training and practice. Practitioner mediators who choose to remain in this stage of their professional development experience their responses to clients becoming patterned and stiff, lacking brilliance or creative potential. These mediators seldom experience the effortless flow that is characteristic of the artist.

Stage Four: The Artist

Artists work with great intention and purpose and are able to call on knowledge and skills in ways that seem intuitive or instinctive. Their accomplishments seem effortless, graceful, agile, and flowing.

Their ease results from a heightened capacity to utilize their abilities. Artists are continually experimenting, testing the reaches of their knowledge and skill. They have the same knowledge and skills as practitioners, but they are inventive, bringing their own interpretation to the application of their knowledge and skills, applying them in novel and unexpected ways. They are inquisitive, seek opportunities to test their knowledge and skills, are open to novelty, have a passion for experimentation, and love to learn. Artists learn from their experiences; they tease out of each event and situation every particle of meaning and understanding. They are creative in their work, not merely functional. Creative practitioners are those "who express unusual thoughts, who are interesting and stimulating . . . people who experience the world in unusual ways . . . and individuals . . . who have changed our culture" (Csikszentmihalyi, 1996, pp. 25–26).

Why Moving Back Is Moving Forward

The process of professional growth is not linear, nor is the end stage static or final. Even accomplished and highly experienced professionals continued to learn, to gain new skills and deepen their understanding of their profession.

Those who attain a measure of artistry in their professional practices do not cease to aspire to excellence. Artistry is a journey, not a destination. Practitioners who aspire to artistry are constantly drawn toward a new vision of what artistry could be. Each new experience of artistry is the basis for another. Learning is continuous and does not cease when professionals attain competence. The process is not unlike certain martial arts in which students achieve distinctions represented by colored belts that identify stages of competency, proficiency, and skill. They travel a predictable and definite path from novice to accomplished practitioner. Having attained the highest distinction, tenth degree black belt, a student returns to the beginning, becoming a novice once again.* This path signifies a commitment to lifelong learning. Returning to the beginner's mind reinforces the notion that one must repeatedly start anew, with a fresh perspective, curiosity, uncertainty, and openness to learning.

Our model of professional development is dynamic because no individual is ever at the same stage continuously. Novices attempting their first mediations can at times (unintentionally and accidentally) manifest the grace and agility that are attributes of an artist. Achieving the flow characteristic of artistry, however, does not signify that one has developed into an artist; nor does such an experience necessarily advance the mediator prematurely along the developmental steps of professional growth. Similarly, artists may experience the uncertainty and awkwardness of the novice when they attempt to use their professional skills and knowledge in an area of practice that is foreign to them. The learning process extends indefinitely, and professionals who are capable of artistry may at times return to a preceding stage as they grapple with a new area of practice, attempt to use new skills, or rely on new theories.

The example of the martial artist illustrates an aspect of the dynamic quality of the four-stage developmental process. Individuals who return to an earlier stage of their professional development bring with them all the skill, experience, and proficiency that characterize their professional work. Not only does each stage build on the preceding stages, but every experience provides an opportunity for growth, development, and ascendancy along the spiral. To take advantage of this dynamic process in order to learn new approaches, methods, principles, and practices, however, requires being willing to suspend past behaviors and approaches, to explore new terrain, and to be curious and open-minded.

---

*We would like to thank Elsbeth McKay for providing this example.

Universal, Not Model Driven

The dynamic four-stage model of professional development can be generalized throughout the field of mediation. Its application is not limited to any particular approach, form, model, or orientation of practice. In recent years, controversy between different approaches to mediation has occupied considerable attention—for example, distinguishing a facilitative orientation from an evaluative orientation. These discussions have stimulated further reflection and analysis among mediators that has resulted in a deeper, richer understanding of the principles and premises of practice. Practitioners have been challenged to identify the theoretical bases from which they operate and to pay attention to the congruence between theory and practice. In Chapter Five we talk further about the constellation of theories and their role in defining mediation practice.

The value of reflective practice and interactive process transcends mediators' particular theoretical orientations, their arenas of practice, and the types and contexts of conflict situations with which they are concerned. These methods and principles have proven useful to mediators who subscribe to evaluative and directive approaches as well as to those who adhere to the transformative approach and the principles of empowerment and recognition. Regardless of theory, context, or arena, the concepts and methods of professional development suggested in this book can support the development of artistry in professional practice or in any other activity.

This model of professional development geared toward artistry has applications and implications for all forms of mediation and for mediators at all levels of training and education. The concepts and practices presented in this book have been incorporated into basic and advanced mediation training, seminars, mediator supervision, and university programs. The systematic and disciplined application of reflective practice and interactive process assists mediators in their journey from the novice to the artist. In the book's concluding chapter, the use of these two processes in mediator education and training are considered in detail.

Artistry as the Integration of Reflective Practice and Interactional Process

Artistry in professional practice is a search for excellence that transcends the boundaries of practice models, has universal applicability in education and training programs, and is the key to professional satisfaction and competence. To attain artistry requires three essential elements: (1) practice skills, (2) theoretical knowledge, and (3) the ability to make useful and appropriate connections between theory and practice. As we described earlier, the path to artistry begins with the acquisition of these essential elements and then proceeds through a series of developmental steps or stages until the professional is able to bring to bear her own unique perspective and interpretation on the problems and situations of professional practice. Without these essential elements, the journey will be short and unsatisfying.

Advancement through the stages of professional development requires the ability and discipline to integrate reflective practice methodology and interactive process. Figure 1.2 depicts the essential connection between these two elements. We do not depict conceptual knowledge and skill competency in this figure because they are prerequisites for attaining artistry and this book does not address the specific areas of knowledge nor the particular techniques required for competent practice.

Reflection

Reflection is the process by which professionals think about the experiences, events, and situations of practice and then attempt to make sense of them in light of the professionals' understanding

Figure 1.2. Reflection and Interaction Lead to Artistry.

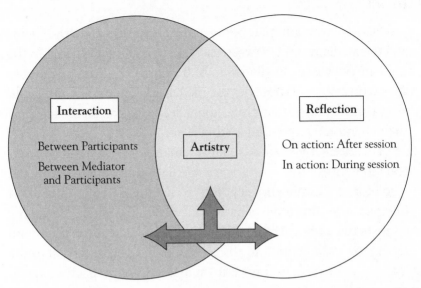

of relevant theory. The objects of reflection are the unique, uncertain nature of a particular situation, the practice skills appropriate to the circumstance, and the constellation of theories that might help explain what is occurring. Mediators first identify an opportunity for reflection by attending to the interactive process and noting critical moments; they then apply the methods of reflective practice.

Reflection occurs both during the performance of professional practice (reflection in action) and after the experience (reflection on action). It nurtures exploration and discoveries that lead to an increased repertoire of skills, it enhances the person's ability to modify forms of intervention, and it may alter his way of thinking about the problems presented. Reflection in action occurs moment to moment during the course of delivering the professional practice. Postsession reflection (reflection on action) may be done either individually or with the help of an instructor, coach, or supervisor.

Interaction

Interaction is the interplay between the clients, between the clients and the mediator, and between each client and the mediator. In the interactive process, mediators look at how their clients respond to the techniques and strategies the mediators employ. In turn, mediators consider how their professional decisions are affected by how their clients are responding to them.

The interactive process requires a microfocus, attending to critical moments in the course of the mediation. Doing so allows the mediator to identify choice points, to see these small moments of interaction as indicative of and connected to the whole. Becoming aware of these critical moments, making deliberate use of them, and seeing their connection to the overall process are essential to the interactive process. In these critical moments of interaction, mediators apply the principles and methods of reflective practice and thus make choices about the direction and focus of the mediation.

Essential Elements: Foundation in Skills and Knowledge

The journey from novice to artist depends on the individual obtaining a foundation in the essential skills and conceptual underpinnings of practice. Without such skills and knowledge, mediators will be limited in their professional development; they will not advance beyond the apprentice stage. Without the ability to communicate clearly and effectively, to listen attentively, to ask helpful and timely questions, and to carry out myriad other tasks associated with the mediation process, the practitioner is limited in the ability to move along the developmental path. Mediators who lack key practice skills will have limited success, and despite effort, enthusiasm, and commitment they will remain locked into one of the early stages of development.

Theory is the foundation of professional practice; it is the ground on which mediators stand, the basis for making choices about the timing and implementation of strategies and techniques. Understanding which theories influence and shape professional practice enables mediators to initiate interventions that are purposeful and directed toward an identified goal, and provides a basis for them to interpret and evaluate responses to their interventions. Practitioners who lack a grounding in theory do not have the ability to evaluate and assess their interventions with clients. Their choice of techniques is reactive rather than responsive. Without a conceptual foundation, they lack the ability to duplicate an experience or to translate knowledge and skills from one arena of practice into another.

Professional competence is characterized in part by the extent to which the mediator identifies the theoretical bases for the application of skills to address a problem situation and then designs and implements approaches consistent with those theories. The ability to make these connections, to integrate theory and practice, is a hallmark of the competent professional and an element required for the mediator's journey toward artistry.

Walking the Path of Artistry

Before you leave this chapter, complete the following activity:

Recall a time when you were successful in your professional practice, when you felt particularly competent and capable, when you were working at a very high level of skill. For the purposes of this exercise, success does not necessarily imply that the parties resolved their conflict or reached an agreement on any issue. Note your answers to the following questions:

- What occurred that you would define as successful?
- What was your role in this success story?
- What knowledge was useful in responding to this problem or situation?
- What skills were useful in dealing with this situation?

- Have you received training that would help you to understand and respond to this situation?
- What professional experience helped you deal with this situation?

Compare your answers with the elements of artistry described in this chapter.

Looking Back, Looking Forward

The path of professional development leads from novice through apprentice and practitioner to artist. The journey begins with the novice stage, a time of enthusiasm, inquisitiveness, and curiosity. The novice is a mimic, modeling his behavior on that of his instructors. Apprentices have gained rudimentary skills and basic knowledge; they test their abilities in practice settings, becoming more adept and skilled. The practitioner is an accomplished professional, able to use a wide range of skills and strategies with purpose and effect. The artist, like the novice, has a beginner's mind—open, curious, seeking new ideas and information. In addition, the artist is able to bring her own interpretation to the practices of the profession.

Artistry is achieved by first gaining a basic understanding of the conceptual foundations of the field of practice, and the ability to utilize an array of practice skills. With these essential elements as a basis, artistry can be achieved through the application of the methods and principles of reflective practice and interactive process. Building on the description of artistry provided in this chapter, we next consider the six hallmarks of artistry, the features and behaviors that define and characterize an artist's performance. We move from the conceptual to the pragmatic, from the general to the specific.

Chapter Two

The Hallmarks of Artistry

In the preceding chapter, we described the characteristics of artistry and identified the essential elements (skills and knowledge) and foundational processes (reflective practice and interactive process) that support and guide the practitioner along the journey toward artistry. We also described the experience of flow that arises from the expression of artistry—the sense of effortlessness, of timelessness, and of being fully engaged. In this chapter we introduce six hallmarks—sets of language, behaviors, and attitudes—that characterize artistic practice, and through case examples we explore the manifestation of these hallmarks in practice settings. We also look at a number of the barriers to achieving artistry—the signs that a professional is mired in a stage of development and may need to return to an earlier stage in order to find a way out of the morass and back to the path toward artistry.

Artistry does not always appear in the brilliant performance of a talented and exceptional athlete, musician, or mediator. It may also show up in the commonplace experiences of daily life, in practical, routine, and mundane activities. The dazzling performance, no matter how exciting or remarkable, is not always the hallmark that distinguishes the presence of artistry. Whether artistry occurs in the mundane or the sublime, it is that special quality or gift that separates the great from the ordinary, the master from the performer, the distinguished from the conventional, the ingenious response to a problem from the commonplace answer. To understand the experiences that signify artistry, we turn our attention to the behaviors and attitudes, the hallmarks, that characterize artistry.

The expressions of artistry in music, art, and sports are ubiquitous. Whether listening to the extraordinary voice of Kiri Te Kanawa giving expression to an aria, the pulsating beat and powerful lyrics of rap music, or the compelling music and words of the "Ode to Joy" from Beethoven's Ninth Symphony, each of us understands in ways that may be visceral and not at all analytical that we are experiencing artistry. For some people, artistry is embodied in the paintings of the great masters, such as Picasso, Monet, or Rembrandt; for others, the sculptures of Michelangelo and Rodin are the ultimate expression of artistry. Artistry may be defined by the moves of a lithe and graceful gymnast, or in the strength and agility of a dancer. But the criteria by which we measure artistry in these performances are elusive, uncertain, and highly individualized. What to one person seems to be an expression of artistry may to another person seem merely adequate, lacking distinctive qualities. In athletics, artistry is generally determined by performance criteria that are concrete, observable, and measurable. Yet athletes are praised as often for their intensity, attitude, and determination as for their more tangible achievements. In most professions and other endeavors, there are few measures by which artistic performance can be identified and valued. Genius is evident when it appears. Ingenuity, talent, and wisdom are valued. But the qualities that define excellence are elusive. It is a challenge to define and describe the qualities of artistry, to articulate the particular behaviors, language, and attitudes that characterize a performance that is worthy of esteem.

We have developed six hallmarks of artistry in professional mediation practice:

Attention to detail: Responsive in the moment

Curiosity: Open to new perspectives

Exploration and discovery: Not bound by limiting assumptions

Developing and testing formulations: Holding on tightly, letting go lightly

Interpretation: Resilient and flexible

Patience and vision: Balanced between process and outcome

We next describe the attributes of these six hallmarks, then we turn to several examples from mediation cases and training experiences that illustrate the language, behavior, and attitudes characteristic of each attribute.

Hallmark 1. Attention to detail: Responsive in the moment

Artists notice the details. A painter gives attention not only to the color, perspective, and design of a piece but also to the location, lighting, and setting for its display. Musicians are concerned with the acoustics and other elements that affect performance, such as the care of their instruments, as well as with musical technique and execution. In each instance, what distinguishes the exceptional from the ordinary is not simply the quality of the performance itself (the painting or music) but the subtle elements that enhance and enrich the performance. For the mediator as well, attention to detail typifies artistic performance. Mediators demonstrate artistry by observing nuances in the parties' behavior and their reactions to one another, and by noticing subtle shifts in language or tone of voice.

Many mediators attempt to gauge the direction of the mediation and plan several moves in advance. They are looking toward the next step, knowing that such planning allows them to organize, manage, and direct the process. They frame issues and design a series of interventions intended to move the process forward constructively. Artistic mediators are continually observing behavioral and language clues, which are often subtle and elusive, that indicate the need for attention and response.

This is not to suggest that artistic mediators are so obsessed with or slavishly attentive to detail, so closely monitoring the moment-to-moment behaviors, that they lose sight of the overall process. Like the photographer who surveys a scene, takes in the entire view, and then selects one portion as the subject for the photograph, the mediator maintains an awareness of the larger picture while simultaneously shifting focus between particular aspects of the interaction. The details of these interactions reveal critical moments, cues, or circumstances that require attention and possibly a response. The artistic mediator attends to the critical moments and fashions responses as appropriate.

The following examples are taken from simulated mediation sessions conducted in our classes, workshops, and supervision meetings.

Example. Two coworkers whose conflict over working conditions, allocation of assignments, and work schedules had deteriorated into name calling and public arguments had nearly reached what appeared to be a complete resolution to their dispute. The mediator reviewed with the parties the terms of their agreement and asked whether they were satisfied that the agreement addressed all their concerns, whether its terms were clear and understandable, and whether they wanted to make any additions or corrections. The disputants confirmed their understanding of the agreement and acknowledged that it resolved all of their outstanding issues. Before concluding the session, the mediator suggested that he meet briefly in caucus with each disputant. In the private session with Agnes (the older of the two disputants), the mediator learned that she suspected Sandi (the other, younger employee) of undermining Agnes's job in order to take over the position. During her private meeting with the mediator, Sandi expressed hope that the agreement would end Agnes's paranoid delusions that Sandi was in competition for Agnes's job. By convening the private sessions, the mediator was able to test his formulation of an incomplete agreement and learned new information that led to further discussions with the parties about Agnes's concerns regarding competition from Sandi.

When the mediator was questioned about offering to meet privately with the parties at what seemed to be the concluding moments of a lengthy mediation, the mediator replied that Agnes's voice had seemed to be wavering as she affirmed the agreement. Her tremulous reply hinted at the possibility that she might not be entirely satisfied with the agreement; her tone suggested unexpressed concerns or reservations. To learn whether these suspicions might be valid, the mediator requested the private sessions so that Agnes might be able to express any misgivings about the agreements and Sandi might be able to confirm that additional issues had not been identified and discussed.

At the moment that the mediation seemed at an end, the mediator was vigilant and observant, noticing and responding to a detail that might easily have been overlooked. The slight tremor in Agnes's voice, likely unnoticeable by a less attentive mediator, provided an important clue that led to the request for private meetings with the parties. And by talking privately with the parties, that mediator learned of additional issues that required attention. Thus he prevented the parties from entering into an agreement that would not have fully resolved the problems between them.

Hallmark 2. Curiosity: Open to new perspectives

Many parties in conflict are so self-absorbed and caught up in their arguments that they are unwilling or unable to hear new or different information that might alter or add to their understanding of the situation. Mediators are also susceptible to the same tunnel vision. In the midst of conflict, disputants experience confusion, uncertainty, and anxiety. They are often preoccupied with satisfying and obtaining their predetermined goals (Bush and Folger, 1994). Such an egocentric, self-centered view of the conflict generally leads to characterizing, stereotyping, or even demonizing the other party as the antagonist or perpetrator. Parties who become locked into such narrow views of the dispute and of the other party typically block out information that contradicts their position. They ignore new information that may help them see the situation through a different lens, reiterating the story of events that tends to reinforce their narrow view of the situation. By this dynamic, each party's perception of the conflict and of the other parties is reconfirmed at every turn.

The artistic mediator attends to the nuances of the parties' interactions and notices when this narrowing occurs. Observing the parties' behavior and language, the mediator recognizes the opportunity to help them enlarge their perspective. At these moments, the mediator makes strategic interventions in order to encourage each disputant to understand the other party's perspective; to take in new ideas, data, or experiences that may alter their understanding of the conflict; to question assumptions about themselves and the other party; and to stimulate the exploration for creative solutions.

Example. Two neighbors were referred to mediation in order to resolve the problem of a large, frisky dog, Buster, who frequently escaped his enclosure and whose enthusiasm (and size) terrified neighborhood children. After inviting the parties to share their perspectives about the incident, the mediator helped them explore a variety of possible solutions to the problem of how to keep Buster contained so he would not frighten the children. Buster's owner and the parent of a child who had been bowled over by Buster during a recent escape from his pen identified, discussed, and eventually rejected the most obvious solutions (such as a stronger gate, a lock on the gate, and keeping Buster in the house when the children were outside). Both parties seemed frustrated by their inability to generate a workable solution.

Observing their diligent but unsuccessful efforts, the mediator turned first to the parent and asked, "Why did you move to this neighborhood?" She explained that she and her family had lived in the city for many years and wanted to be in an area where they could have a yard for the children to play in. They loved the tree-lined streets and the fact that there were other families with children in the neighborhood. Turning to Buster's owner, the mediator asked how long he had lived in the neighborhood. "All my life," he replied, and added that his family had once owned the area that was now clustered with homes in which the woman and man lived."My father had a farm but sold the land when farming became too difficult." At that moment, the parent asked the dog owner,"What was it like here when you were a kid?" From that point the focus shifted away from the problem with Buster to a discussion about life in the neighborhood, returning eventually to a successful resolution of the problem of Buster and the neighborhood children.

With a simple yet elegant question (Why did you move to this neighborhood?), the mediator helped the parties move away from viewing one another simply as disputants trying to solve a nagging problem. They began instead to see each other as neighbors who had something in common—their enjoyment of the neighborhood. The mediator's question opened up the possibility that Buster's owner might be able to understand the parent's perspective and that the parent might have some appreciation for and sensitivity to the dog owner. The shift in their perspectives helped the parties move away from a limited and restricting way of viewing each other, gave them a new understanding of how they each saw the conflict and its context, and stimulated a renewed search for a workable solution to what they now experienced as a shared dilemma.

Hallmark 3. Exploration and discovery: Not bound by limiting assumptions

People use generalizations and create categories in order to understand the world. Colors are categories, as are religions, political parties, type of employment, gender, age, nationality, and marital status. These are times when generalizations are useful for our conceptual understanding of issues. "Categorizing is a fundamental and natural human activity. It is the way we come to know the world" (Langer, 1989, p. 154).We make generalizations and assign people to categories without thinking clearly about whether all people in a certain group share the same characteristics, qualities, or beliefs. For example, someone identified as ascribing to a particular religion may be assumed to have values, beliefs, rituals, and practices similar to those of others of the same faith. In reality, each person is unique, and by assigning people to categories and attributing certain characteristics to them we deny them that individuality.

When these categories take on a life of their own they become stereotypes and can become dysfunctional, even harmful. For instance, when people adhere to such categories despite information that indicates clear distinctions among people in the same category, the opportunity to gain a different and broader perspective is lost. Moreover, when people then operate on the basis of those categorizations, they fail to perceive and respond to important differences. Categorization is not in itself dangerous; what is dangerous is the mindless acceptance of those categories without recognizing that they are not truth but only ideas constructed to help us make sense of the world.

In the drama of conflict, disputants tend toward simplistic and generally rigid characterizations of themselves (just, receptive, responsible, worthy, or right) and of the other party (unjust, unwilling to listen, undependable, sinister, or wrong). Becoming attached to categories can often lead to mindless and rigid adherence to a single perspective on a problem, situation, or individual. Becoming locked into one view, unwilling to create new categories for distinguishing features and characteristics, creates the inability to experience a new way of looking at a person, situation, or problem.

Example. A small group of people who worked in a religious institution wanted to revise the bylaws and mission statement of their organization. After struggling with the task and experiencing little success, the members agreed to hire a consultant-mediator to help them identify the issues they needed to consider and to create new ideas that would be cast into new governing documents. The consultant was aware that the group prayed for guidance and for aid in accomplishing the organization's projects and activities. After an opening prayer was offered by the group's leader, the consultant offered a story to the group. The story was about a monastery that had fallen on hard times. In an effort to find a solution to the decline of the monastery's fortunes, the abbot sought advice from a nearby cleric of a different faith who offered hope by suggesting that the monastery's residents behave toward one another as if any one of them might be the Messiah. As a result of its residents treating one another with reverence and love, the monastery again flourished.

The group of disputants found solace and joy in this idea. The discussion about the bylaws and mission statement was abandoned in favor of a conversation among the group's members about the importance of religion in their lives. They bemoaned the lack of time allotted in their busy schedules for talking with one another about their beliefs, the role of God in their lives, and the importance of prayer. They put aside the mission statement and focused instead on devising a plan for worshiping, studying, and praying together.

The mediator, sensitive to the values of the disputants, used the story to acknowledge that the group's discussions were rooted in the members' religious beliefs. The mediator also understood that the group members' goal was not merely to restructure the governing documents but to search for and express a shared understanding of the group's purposes. By telling the story, the mediator responded to the grounding principles of the group, to their devotion to religious belief and practice. Acknowledging the fundamental values that infused the group, the mediator helped the members enlarge their view of the problems that had led to their decision to rework their mission statement and bylaws. They had focused on these documents as the source of their problems; the solution therefore lay in revising the language. The mediator's story motivated the group members to question their assumptions about the source of their difficulties. In doing so they realized that they had defined the problem too narrowly, that by looking at the governing documents they were focusing on the wrong issues. The source of their dilemma was in themselves—in their failure to meet their commitment to one another as spiritually directed people.

Hallmark 4. Developing and testing formulations: Holding on tightly, letting go lightly

Mediators are trained to listen to disputants, to observe their interactions, to develop formulations (hypotheses), and then to design a process that will constructively respond to the conflict. This phenomenon of seeking meaning in a collection of facts is not unique to mediators. Lawyers gather data and frame issues that conform to established causes of action; physicians use their observations of patients and test results to form a diagnosis. Generating a coherent structure of meaning out of what the senses experience is a common practice. Humans classify, pigeonhole, sort, frame, identify, and diagnose—all ways of explaining or giving structure and understanding to sets of information. Once a classification or formulation or diagnosis is formed, people focus on data that tend to confirm their beliefs and conclusions (see Hallmark 2). Viewing an image through the lens of a camera limits one's field of vision; the camera sees only a portion of what the eyes can take in. Like the lens of a camera, humans often focus on only one portion of an image, effectively determining and delimiting what they will or will not see. Sometimes, no matter how well grounded in observation and experience their choices are, they necessarily limit what is viewed as important and relevant. The process of organizing data into constructs that give the data shape and meaning is essential and natural. However, such formulations carry the risk that other useful information may be ignored.

Although all mediators are prone to this risk, artistic practitioners find ways to circumvent this thought trap. They are distinguished by their curiosity and openness to the possibility that their way of framing the conflict, their formulations, may not be suitable or accurate. Using the process of *experimentation* (see Schön, 1983), they constantly question the validity of their formulations. Experimentation has two principal forms: implementing an intervention and observing the responses of the parties, and asking questions of the parties to elicit their view of the conflict situation. This process provides a check and balance on mediators' thinking that minimizes the prospect of being bound by a single, limited perspective. The mediator's discipline is to test, examine, and rework their formulation of the conflict in conjunction with and in response to the way the disputants view the dispute. Vital to the success of a mediation is not only the ability of mediators to form and test formulations, but also their willingness to abandon a frame that is not accurate and responsive. The aphorism we use to characterize this hallmark is, *Hold on tightly, let go lightly*. Be intentional and disciplined in developing formulations, and unrestrained in releasing them when necessary.

Example. A mediator was confronted with allegations of inappropriate sexual contact brought by a coworker (Amy) against her colleague (Bill). Amy and Bill worked closely together, but a recent incident had jeopardized their working relationship. Initially, the mediator viewed the mediation as an effort by the disputants to find a workable solution for a difficult, sensitive, and troubling conflict. The mediator's formulation suggested that mutual misunderstanding led to the incident and that subsequent miscommunication compounded the problem. In developing this formulation or frame for the conflict, the mediator had relied on information provided first by the parties' supervisor and subsequently by the parties. Based on this information as well as on certain assumptions about this type of conflict, the mediator developed her formulation and, to experiment, met separately with Amy and then with Bill.

During her private session with Amy, the mediator asked what Amy hoped to achieve through the mediation. Amy's response was surprising. Angry and hurt that Bill had kissed her without warning or consent, Amy simply wanted an apology and an explanation. She believed that she and Bill could work together in the future, but she needed to regain a sense of trust, so she wanted Bill to acknowledge the problems his rash actions had caused. This information challenged the mediator's formulation and presented an opportunity to adopt a new frame. Having developed a hypothesis grounded in her previous experience with cases of sexual harassment and in certain information she had gathered, the mediator had proceeded according to her understanding of the conflict. She was now confronted with new information that challenged her formulation; she could use this data to revise her formulation or she could ignore the information. The artistic mediator does not hold fast to her original assumptions but shifts her view to match the formulation presented by the parties.

Hallmark 5. Interpretation: Resilient and flexible

Artists interpret; they use their knowledge, skill, and experience in responding to the unique circumstances of each situation to create a performance that is distinct and individual. The notes and notations of a Mozart concerto do not vary, yet the musician brings to the music her special and distinct interpretation and thus creates an original performance. While all performances will have similar components, follow the same form, and rely on the same text, they are never the same. The unique circumstances of the moment infuse the performance with subtle nuances and a distinctive resonance. The result appears flowing, effortless, and intuitive.

Artistic mediators also bring a unique and personal interpretation to their practices. This is not merely a matter of personal style, although the expression is unique to each mediator; and it is more than being resourceful, although being clever and inventive are valued attributes. The artistic mediator creates interventions that are uniquely attuned to the situation and the parties, and implements them with elegance and confidence. She has an ineffable ability to notice and respond to surprising circumstances, and the capacity to be resilient and flexible. These are hallmarks of artistry.

Resilience requires the capacity to respond flexibly without yielding ground. Like the birch tree that bends in a strong wind but does not break, the artistic mediator responds to the events and circumstances of the moment without losing sight of the objectives and purposes of the process.

Example. The unwed parents of an infant child were struggling with whether and under what limitations the father, who had been in prison when the child was born, would be able to visit his daughter. The parents had spoken with but not seen each other for several months preceding the mediation. As the mediator began the introduction, explaining confidentiality and other topics, the parties seemed distracted, inattentive, and anxious. The mediator noticed their behavior, and rather than proceed in the face of their apparent inability to attend to the opening statement, he asked the parties a question, "What do you each hope can be achieved in mediation?" Each parent, having been offered the opportunity to talk about the conflict situation, responded with deep emotion. Eager to tell their stories, the parties became animated and engaged. Later, after both parties had talked about their daughter and their desire to be active and caring parents, the mediator presented the balance of the opening statement.

Mediators learn to deliver an opening statement that contains a number of elements, including discussion of confidentiality, the potential and limitations of the mediation process, the role of the mediator, and in some cases, ground rules. Some mediators rely on a script or a list of items they want to discuss during the opening stage of the mediation, and they deliver it faithfully, in a patterned if cordial manner. Regardless of the parties' behavior, these mediators conscientiously perform the ritual of the opening statement. Mediators who practice in an artistic manner are not bound by a script; they understand the importance of conveying this information to the parties and ensuring that they understand and agree to the conditions for mediation. In the example, the mediator noticed that the parties were distracted and inattentive during the opening statement, so he adjusted to the new circumstances and deferred portions of the opening statement to a later time. The artistic mediator is flexible, resilient, and responsive, able to shift his approach without losing sight of the content of or reasons for the opening statement.

Hallmark 6. Patience and vision: Balanced between process and outcome

For many mediators, regardless of their approach to practice, reaching an agreement is the primary and sometimes sole measure of their success. The parties, too, are understandably eager to reach an outcome; they want a quick resolution to the conflict and often ask how long the process will take. Artists are not unconcerned about outcome—it is part of their performance, the goal of their efforts. However, artists are also concerned with the process by which that outcome is attained, and they are not easily distracted by the lure of outcome. They are necessarily patient, with a clear notion of the ultimate objective, the result to be achieved. Not unlike a successful gardener, who knows that an abundant harvest requires cultivation of the soil, tending the plants, removal of weeds, and adequate water and fertilizer. Achieving an objective requires planning and preparation—a process. Artistic mediation of the sort we have in mind requires patience and perseverance, attention to details, and a clear sense of direction.

Example. During the first meeting in a divorce mediation, Betty presented to her husband, Howard, a proposal for coparenting the couple's three children that she assured him was "fair, workable, and takes everything into account." Inclined to defer to his wife on such matters, Howard indicated, with some reluctance, that the proposal "probably makes good sense. I guess I can try to live with it, if you think it's best for the children." Satisfied with his reply, Betty assured Howard that it would all work out for the best. Howard nodded his assent. The mediator, noticing Howard's tepid response to Betty's proposal, asked the parties, "I am noticing that Betty proposed a plan and Howard agreed. Is this the way you two generally make decisions?"

Betty replied that while Howard was an active father, she had borne the bulk of the responsibility for parenting the children and therefore had a better idea of what they needed. Howard agreed, but added that he had been as involved with the children as possible given his work schedule. "I've been to every parent-teacher meeting, recital, and sporting event. I've taken them shopping for clothes on occasion. I've read them stories at night. I've been a good father to the children."

Betty, with obvious tenderness, responded, "I know Howard, you are a good father. I just don't know how else to manage the parenting when we're in separate homes. I just thought this made sense."

While an agreement on shared parenting is the parties' goal, the mediator is also concerned with the process by which the parties achieve their objective. Good process generally makes for a good agreement, although it does not ensure one. The aphorism that process and objective are invariably linked may not always prove accurate. The mediator must be simultaneously attentive to the parties' objective—reaching a workable parenting plan—and to the value of a process that encourages open, complete, and candid discussions about the nature, design, and details of such a plan. Not rushing to accept the apparent agreement, concerned as much about the journey as about the destination, the mediator patiently encourages the parties to talk about the process by which they will make their decisions.

Returning to an Earlier Stage of Professional Development

Artistry appears when a mediator manifests one or more of the hallmarks just described. Our model of professional development posits a dynamic and continuing process. Artistry is not a static condition that, once attained, is continually present; rather, it is an ongoing exploration of the aspiration for excellence. Artistry can be experienced with increasing frequency if the mediator adopts the principles and methods of interactive process and reflective practice.

Of great importance is recognizing the signs that might indicate that a mediator should return to an earlier stage of development in order to sustain the dynamic process of professional evolution. The following indicators suggest that a mediator may need to develop new practice skills, polish her techniques, or gain additional knowledge:

- Being bound by limiting assumptions
- Failure to take in new information
- Inability (or unwillingness) to reflect on action
- Fixed on outcome
- Inattention to parties
- Mimicry
- Unwillingness to self-reflect
- Inattention to process

Following are examples of these indicators in action.

The Practitioner

A conflict between Jeanne and Daniel escalated to the point that Jeanne put her hands on Daniel's chest to prevent him from coming closer to her. During separate premediation conversations, both Jeanne and Daniel indicated that their behavior had resulted from the intensity of the moment and did not represent a pattern. Neither had been injured and neither expressed a present fear of the other. The mediator, an experienced practitioner, was obsessed with the possibility that the woman would be less able to participate in the mediation until the issue of safety was addressed. In the initial joint meeting, the mediator repeatedly asked Jeanne whether she feared retaliation from Daniel. Jeanne replied no to each question, but with increasing uneasiness.

During a debriefing of this mediation simulation, Jeanne reported that the mediator's repeated questions about her sense of fear caused her to worry that the mediator had learned something from Daniel that would cause Jeanne distress if she knew what it was. Before the mediation she had not felt any concern that Daniel might physically harm her, but the mediator's attention to the issue of her safety caused Jeanne to question her perceptions of Daniel. The mediator denied that he had unreasonably focused on this issue. Despite repeated assurances from Jeanne that her anxiety was exclusively the product of his questions, the mediator was unwilling to consider the possibility that he had become so focused on this one issue that he had interfered with the parties' ability to proceed with the mediation process.

What are the signs that this mediator needs to return to an earlier stage of professional development?

Being bound by limiting assumptions. The mediator believed (as an element of his constellation of theory) that women who have been touched in anger are abused, that abused women are at risk of further injury, and that because continuing harm is possible, abused women may be less able to participate in mediation. Learning of the physical contact between the parties, the mediator developed a formulation that Jeanne was at risk of further injury. This assumption led him to focus on her safety to the exclusion of other issues, despite assurances from Jeanne that she did not fear Daniel. The mediator ignored information that contradicted his formulation.

Failure to take in new information. By interpreting Daniel's behavior as evidence of abuse in the face of contradictory information, the mediator closed off other possible interpretations of the behavior, such as that the shoving was a product of zealous and intense conflict and was not perceived by Jeanne as abusive.

Inability (or unwillingness) to reflect on action. When invited by the teacher and the role-players to consider that his focus on the potential for future harm had clouded his vision and thus interfered with the parties' interest in dealing with the conflict, the mediator was closed to the possibility that he had made a mistake. He defended himself and was unwilling to examine his analysis and conclusions. As a result, he lost an opportunity to learn from the experience.

Even experienced professionals sometimes err; they become fixated on one view of the conflict, on a single, rigid formulation, and that perspective becomes the basis for their interventions. To learn from this example the mediator would benefit from an understanding of and experience in utilizing the methods of reflective practice. Through reflection on action, this mediator would be able to identify the assumptions that led to his formulation, and to understand why he disregarded information from Jeanne that contradicted his hypothesis about the conflict. The reflective process would also help the mediator to learn the importance of remaining open, flexible, and attentive to details.

The Novice

In demonstrating the opening statement during a basic mediation training course, one of the trainees talked for ten to fifteen minutes without interruption. He covered the usual topics of confidentiality, mediation process, role of the mediator, and ground rules. The teacher stopped the mediation to ask the parties about what they had heard in the mediator's opening statement. Each of the parties replied, "Nothing; I was so anxious about being in the mediation and dealing with the other person, all I could think of was what I was going to say. I don't know what the mediator said." The teacher also observed that one of the role-players had even turned her body away from the mediator and was looking out a window.

When asked about the role-players' reactions to his opening statement, the mediator expressed surprise, confusion, and disappointment. He said, "I was focused on what I wanted to accomplish. I wanted to make sure I covered all the points, so I kept my attention on the list of tasks. I didn't even notice that she had turned away from me."

What are the signs that this mediator needs to return to an earlier stage of professional development?

Fixed on outcome. When mediators become so engrossed in the tasks at hand or attracted to the outcome of an intervention, their attention is fixed on the goal. They ignore the details, the behavior and language that might signal the need to direct their attention elsewhere. The process of mediation, the steps along the path, is as critical as the destination.

Inattention to parties. The mediator clearly ignored the signals from one of the role-players as she turned her body away and gazed out a window. The mediator should be aware of interactions not only between the parties but also between each party and the mediator. Being attentive to moment-to-moment shifts in language, behavior, tone of voice, and other indicators helps the mediator identify the signals that a shift in approach is required. In addition to learning to notice such shifts during the mediation, this student mediator may also want to develop a repertoire of responses—ways of attending to these behavioral changes.

Following a script. Effective mediators must understand the rationale for and the tasks of the opening statement, develop skill in presenting the topics, and learn how to respond to questions from the participants. Many beginning mediators follow a checklist or script, parroting the approach their teacher demonstrated. Following a pattern is a problem when it interferes with the mediator's ability to shift away from the script when compelling circumstances require an alteration in a carefully planned presentation.

The Apprentice

The students in an advanced mediation training course conducted a simulated mediation with faculty supervision. The mediator had completed a basic mediation training program and had participated in many mediations, either individually or as a co-mediator. The dispute concerned a homeowner and a contractor hired to construct a room addition. The specific issues were the price for certain extra items, whether the homeowner had authorized the purchase of those items, and the cost for remedying an unanticipated problem with the existing plumbing system. In all, the disputed amount was less than $1,200, or 10 percent of the total budget for the project. Proceeding on the assumption that the issues were exclusively economic and that compromise was the most reasonable approach to dealing with such a conflict, the mediator talked with the parties in a series of private sessions. She used the caucus with the contractor to persuade him to make a swift settlement, to cut his losses in order to avoid the time and expense of litigation. In caucus with the homeowner, the mediator encouraged her to see that she was getting full value for her money and that a compromise settlement was the best possible outcome.

When asked following the exercise what had led her to use private meetings to deal with the conflict, the mediator answered that she did not think it made sense "to spend much time on such a small amount of money." She believed she could get them to a settlement if she could talk with each person separately. The role-players, when asked about the experience, expressed frustration at being kept in separate rooms, unable to talk with one another; they had expected mediation to give them a chance to talk with each other. One role-player remarked that he had asked during a caucus whether he could talk directly with the other person, but the mediator had not responded to his question. When asked about the role-players' comments, the mediator reiterated that in her experience, parties were more likely to reach settlements in economic disputes when the mediator worked with them in caucus. In response to a question from the faculty supervisor about situations when the use of private sessions for economic disputes might not be appropriate, the mediator indicated that there might be such instances, but she always used this technique.

What are the signs that this mediator needs to return to an earlier stage of professional development?

Mimicry. Too often, an apprentice models an approach demonstrated by a teacher, following a pattern without regard for the appearance of clues that might suggest that a different approach is warranted. Even when the circumstances appear to be similar to other situations in which a particular approach was successful, the artistic mediator must mindfully design interventions appropriate to the unique circumstances. Learning to reflect in action will help this mediator avoid the peril of applying the same technique without considering the uniqueness of each situation.

Unwillingness to self-reflect. As the conversation between the teacher and mediator indicates, this student believed she had the right answer and was not open to considering new information. Believing that she had all the data necessary, the mediator deflected and ignored information that might provide a clearer view and a broader perspective.

Inattention to process. As we see from this mediator's failure to respond to the parties' requests to engage directly, she is inattentive to details. Artistry requires the ability to be mindfully attuned to the moment-to-moment shifts in the parties' behaviors, attitudes, language, and interactions while also maintaining a global view of the mediation process.

Walking the Path of Artistry

Begin by thinking of a situation that you found particularly puzzling (for whatever reasons)—an event within a mediation that you found surprising or perplexing. Note the words and behaviors—the nature of the interactions—that were the source of your uncertainty. Then list the six hallmarks and make two columns, one in which to indicate that you have met the criteria of the hallmark and the other in which to indicate a need to return to a former stage of professional development. Reflecting on the case you have identified, mark the appropriate column. Complete this exercise for several situations and see whether a pattern emerges that might point you toward further reflection, training, coaching, or reading.

Looking Back, Looking Forward

Beginning with a broad, conceptual definition of artistry, we have identified the characteristic behaviors and attitudes, the hallmarks, that distinguish artistry in professional practice. The various examples illustrate the manifestation of these hallmarks. We are gradually moving from the conceptual to the concrete, from abstract notions about a mysterious quality known as artistry, to specific skills, techniques, and strategies that embody artful practice.

In the next chapter we present the practical steps leading to artistry in practice. We explore the methods by which mediators can learn the discipline, skills, principles, and practices that lead to artistry.

Chapter Three

Integrating Artistry into Practice

Chapters One and Two defined the characteristics and hallmarks of artistry in professional mediation practice. With that as groundwork, we now consider how mediators move along the path from novice to artist, and we describe the process by which they learn the methods, techniques, principles, and behaviors that foster an artistic practice, that signify exceptional ability, and that characterize this unique approach to the problems of professional practice. We also describe instructional methods that we believe significantly increase opportunities for professionals to advance along the developmental path.

Artistry Is Learnable

As we noted earlier, artistry is learnable. Notwithstanding the subjective, intangible nature of artistic practice, we believe that its principles can be identified, learned, integrated, and re-created for others to experience. Each person is capable of experiencing artistry in his or her endeavors.

This chapter describes the learning process, the method by which professionals develop the necessary knowledge, skills, and habits to become artists. Many of the basic practice skills that we identify as essential for professional development are not unusual; most mediators learn them in beginning and advanced mediation training programs. The core areas of knowledge are also likely to be familiar to most mediators; they are the canons, the fundamental principles and beliefs that support practice. What is unique about our approach is the process by which the mediator synthesizes knowledge and skills—through reflective practice and the interactive process.

Most mediators have learned a variety of practice skills and techniques, such as active listening, clarifying and framing issues, problem solving, building agreements, and developing rapport and trust. Students are aware that mastering these skills is essential to their success as mediators, and both educators and students focus on the acquisition of these skills. In addition, each area and context of mediation practice—from community to family to commercial to public policy disputes—has uniquely structured approaches, techniques, and strategies. As mediators move through the stages of professional development, they acquire an increasing variety and number of these practice tools.

Educators and trainers present mediators with the fundamental principles of mediation and the concepts that shape the profession. The knowledge required for competent practice includes such topics as the nature of conflict and its sources, individual and group responses to conflict, mediation as a professional practice within the legal system, professional standards for mediators, cultural concerns and implications, the reasons for and role of confidentiality, and barriers to and motivation for cooperation. This list is illustrative, not inclusive. Moreover, each area of mediation practice contains further specialized areas of knowledge.

The Academy of Family Mediators has produced a list, several pages in length, of topics from many areas that must be covered in a training program to meet the academy's standards. Competent practice requires understanding the fundamental concepts and principles and practicing the essential skills. Students who complete a forty-hour introductory mediation training program generally acquire solid grounding in these core areas. The acquisition of such knowledge and skills, however, provides a limited and basic foundation for practice. Courses must also instill in students a sense of what mediation practice entails—of what it is like to be a mediator.

Students who complete basic skills training are generally well settled in the novice stage of professional development. They have attained a basic skill level and have begun to acquire a body of knowledge about the profession. These trainees have advanced from a stage where they were largely unaware of what they knew and what they needed to know to a stage where they have an elementary understanding of the profession and of the skills and knowledge required of a mediator. They are self-conscious in their approach to practice. Mediators at this stage of professional development are spirited learners, eager to gain experience, to build their skills, and to learn more about the process of mediation. The enthusiasm of the novice mediator is perhaps best exemplified by the number of questions they ask of teachers and coaches.

Advancing from novice to apprentice, the mediator acquires more experience, often in a co-mediation setting. Learning by doing is central to the development of the apprentice mediator. In such a setting, the mediator tries out an array of practice skills, thus building her repertoire. Apprentices gain a deeper understanding of the profession and of their role, thus augmenting their knowledge and strengthening their skills. The apprentice is an earnest, passionate learner and continues to discover new aspects of the profession.

Practitioners, those professionals with considerable experience and education, are capable, resourceful, and effective. They are losing their self-consciousness about their practice. Their work is conducted largely in a poised and seemingly effortless manner. Practitioners may continue to discover new approaches through reflective process, but for many practitioners the level of and passion for exploration have diminished.

We believe that mediators will not move beyond the practitioner stage unless they develop the discipline and practices of reflection. The ability to learn from each experience; to refine, adjust, and enhance one's skills; and to respond thoughtfully to the unique and surprising events in professional practice can be achieved through the consistent, thoughtful, and intentional application of the methods and principles of reflective practice. The fusion of reflective practice, described thoroughly in Chapter Six, and the interactive process, dealt with in Chapter Seven, enhances the capacity for artistry.

What distinguishes musicians who can perform a piece of music with competence and accuracy, who can create a dazzling performance by bringing their own interpretation to the music? The person with such seemingly ineffable qualities is noticeable—the artist among the practitioners, the genius among the talented, the exceptional among the capable. We know artistry when we hear the music, see the performance, taste the meal, or watch the ball game. We now explore a number of examples that illustrate both the qualities of artistry and the process that supports its development.

The Reflective Practicum

The following three case examples are taken from training and coaching sessions that illustrate the process by which mediators develop their knowledge and skills and advance through the developmental stages. In these examples, we develop further the notion that artistry is learnable, that it is possible to synthesize talents, gifts, knowledge, and skills through the principles and methods we describe. The examples provide an opportunity to see both the development of artistry and the type of coaching that is most likely to produce it. They illustrate both the temperament and the skills of artistry. Artistry requires not merely the ability to manifest excellent performance; it also requires an aspirational mind-set—an inclination toward excellence, the desire to improve and to be a lifelong learner. Artistry is evidenced by behavior, but it also requires an attitude, a way of viewing oneself as a professional. The examples we present therefore not only identify the behaviors, skills, and methods by which a professional moves in this direction, but they also highlight the disposition toward learning that characterizes the artist. In each instance, the exchanges occurred during a mediation role-play. In the discussion of each case, we first present the background, followed by the conversation between the mediator and the clients, and then the dialogue between the mediator and the coach that occurred during the postmediation debriefing. In conclusion, we interpret each case in light of the aspiration toward artistry.

Example 1: Sally and Bob

Sally, a seventeen-year-old who lived with her father, wanted to move from the family home into an apartment that she would share with several friends in her age range. Sally's parents (Barbara and Bob) had been separated for nine months and Barbara lived forty miles from Bob and Sally.

During the early stages of the mediation, following a number of emotional exchanges between Sally and her dad in which they restated their positions with increasing conviction and raised voices, Sally, exasperated, told Bob that she wanted to move out in order "to be with people who understand me." The mediator (a practitioner) asked Bob to repeat what he had heard Sally say. Bob responded, "She said she wants to be with her friends and that I don't talk with her." Turning to Sally, the mediator asked whether Bob had understood her. Sally said, "I can't talk with my dad anymore." Inviting Bob's further comment, the mediator asked what he made of Sally's last statement, and Bob answered, "I guess I haven't been very available to Sally."

The conversation between the coach and the mediator that followed these exchanges focused on how the marital separation had affected both Sally and Bob.

> *Coach:* What was your hypothesis about this conflict?
>
> *Mediator:* At first I thought this was another conflict that involved a teenager asserting her desire for autonomy—very natural at her age—and a father who was trying to assert his parental role. I also considered the possibility that Sally was reacting to the loss of her mother, and that Bob wanted to avoid losing another woman in his life.

Coach: What did you do to experiment, to test out your hypothesis?

Mediator: I listened to the talk between them, and they were repeating their original positions—"I want to move out," "No, you can't." They seemed to be doing in the mediation what they had been doing at home—talking and not listening to one another—so I asked Bob to repeat what Sally had said.

Coach: And what did you learn from the exchanges between Bob and Sally that followed?

Mediator: That they weren't talking with one another at home, and Bob acknowledged that he hadn't been available for Sally. The fact that they then began talking more with each other suggested that one of the problems that likely caused this conflict was that they weren't spending time talking together.

Coach: And if the mediation had continued, what would you have done next to pursue your sense of what contributed to their conflict?

Mediator: I would have asked about the time prior to the separation, whether they were able to talk then, and I would have learned more about their lives prior to the conflict.

Coach: And what do you hope this line of inquiry would have produced?

Mediator: While I don't have any idea whether they would ever see one another's point of view about Sally's moving out, I think if they had a chance to talk about how things have changed in the past nine months, they might find that they have some common ground—their losses.

Coach: And why would this be important in terms of the mediation?

Mediator: I believe that if parties to a conflict have a chance to find something in common, it gives them the basis for talking about their differences.

This exchange in many respects exhibits an adequate, thoughtful, and skillful way to respond to the parties and their conflict; it is clearly competent work. What behaviors, attitude, and approach distinguish this example from others of equal aptitude and skill? What hallmarks are represented? Finally, what coaching techniques were used by the teacher?

The student mediator has demonstrated three of the hallmarks of artistry in this mediation and debriefing: reflection in action, hypothesis generation and experimentation, and resilience and flexibility.

Reflection in Action. In this brief example, the student mediator demonstrated one of the traits of reflective practice: *reflection in action* (Schön, 1983, 1987). She began with a formulation, based on her observations of what happened in the mediation, that Bob and Sally were carrying out in the session a pattern they had developed over some time—talking at rather than listening to one another. With the assistance of the coach, the student mediator examined what occurred during the mediation, reflected on her thought process as she engaged with the clients, probed to determine whether her intervention approaches were congruent with her framing of the conflict, and considered what other formulations or interventions might have been appropriate and useful. The intention of the exercise of reflection is to look back at the experience and, by examining the mediator's behavior in the session, to gain an understanding of what techniques she used, when, and why, and what responses she received. On the basis of this information, the mediator can identify what occurred and attempt to explain why.

Forming and Testing Hypotheses. The mediator listened attentively to the parties' conversation and formed a working formulation that might explain part of the conflict, asking herself whether there was an explanation for why Bob and Sally were in conflict. What was occurring in their lives that could generate conflict, and why had the issue of Sally's leaving home arisen? The mediator then experimented, patiently testing her formulation through questions addressed to Bob and Sally. Assessing her formulation in light of the parties' responses to her questions, the mediator considered other possible explanations for the conflict. She wondered about the possibility that this situation represented a "conflict that involved a teenager asserting her desire for autonomy—very natural at her age—and a father who was trying to assert his parental role," and she looked at the possibility that the conflict grew out of the father and daughter's mutual loss of the mother-wife.

The mediator listened to the parties and heard them repeatedly assert their positions in ways that suggested to her that the parties were not listening to one another, either in the mediation session or at home. Therefore her frame for the conflict shifted, her formulation was reformed, and she tested out the new explanation for the conflict by asking Bob to restate what he heard Sally saying. This intervention proved quite successful. As they responded to the mediator's questions, Bob and Sally progressed from talking at one another to talking with one another; they set aside the original problem that brought them to mediation and focused on the common experience of loss.

Testing her formulation also prevented the mediator from becoming locked into a too narrow perspective on the conflict. Witnessing the verbal duel between Bob and Sally, the mediator might have concluded that the conflict over Sally's moving out was the enactment of an archetypal struggle between a child eager to demonstrate her maturity and a parent determined to rein in his daughter's rush toward adulthood. Although the conflict might have exhibited such characteristics, the mediator was careful to avoid becoming attached to any single explanation for the parties' behavior, and by continually generating and testing formulations, the mediator engaged the parties, invited their participation in the exploration of their conflict, and searched for an explanation that was theoretically sound and grounded in the parties' experiences.

The mediator's interventions were distinguished by her ability to be purposeful in her actions. At all times she knew what she was doing, and why; she evaluated the success of her interventions by measuring the parties' interactions against what she predicted was likely to occur based on her formulation. Having constructed an initial explanation—a formulation—for the conflict, the mediator remained open to the possibility of other interpretations, to new ideas about how the parties viewed the conflict. In this way she avoided the all-too-common mistake of forming a judgment about the conflict and then managing the mediation as though there were no other possible explanation.

In addition, the mediator demonstrated the value of being in the moment, attentive to what is happening between the parties and (although in this case it was less important) between each disputant and the mediator. Attending to the interactions, the mediator noted when critical moments arose, when she should be particularly attentive and responsive. She did not become overly invested in her own view of the conflict, even though her formulation might have reasonably explained the conflict. Rather, she listened to the parties, engaged them in a process of experimentation, and responded according to their perceptions, attitudes, and behaviors. Developing a formulation requires a broad view of the parties and their conflict; assessing the validity of that formulation requires attention to detail.

Coaching. Of the instructional methods employed by coaches, the most important in the development of artistry is the use of elicitive questions (see also the example of elicitive questioning in Chapter Six). The elicitive approach is grounded in the belief that the coach is a catalyst for the mediator's learning and that the mediator's knowledge is a resource for learning (Lederach, 1995). The goal of this approach is to nurture exploration and discovery by the mediator, who is encouraged to reflect on the experiences of the mediation role-play. In ways that parallel our notions about how reflective practitioners bring their expertise to the mediation process (see discussion in Chapter Six), the coach and the mediator each bring their knowledge, experience, and creativity to the coaching-learning process.

Contrasting the elicitive approach with a more traditional method of coaching, the prescriptive approach, which is widely used by mediation instructors, illustrates the importance of elicitive methods (Lederach, 1995). Coaches who rely on the prescriptive approach see themselves as experts in a particular model or style of mediation and as having specialized knowledge or expertise to share with students. The design and structure of the learning process is directed by the coach, including the approach, pace, and focus of the learning activities. The coach's task is to shape the mediator's practice to meet the requirements of a particular form of mediation. The methods used in the prescriptive approach include identifying the mediator's needs, demonstrating the correct technique or the proper application of the technique, and analyzing and criticizing a particular intervention. In the prescriptive method, the mediator is the receptacle for learning, the object of the lessons. This method is grounded in the coach's belief that he or she is the expert and the mediator is the vessel into which learning is poured.

Coaching that leads to artistry, conversely, is an interactive process in which the coach asks questions that encourage mediators to uncover for themselves what was successful or unsuccessful, and to identify possible explanations for the parties' responses to the mediator's approach. The coach supports learning by helping mediators identify the reasoning behind their strategies and approaches, and by having them consider the impact of their interventions on the disputants. Elicitive coaching helps make visible the process of experimentation and is itself a model for the process of reflection in action.

Elicitive questions stimulate the mediator to contemplate, to examine the experiences of the mediation. They help the mediator develop the habits of reflective practice, the disciplines of reflecting in action and reflecting on action. In addition to asking questions about the mediator's formulation and the experiments she conducted, the coach in this case explored the mediator's perceptions and conclusions by asking such questions as, "What did you learn from the exchanges between Bob and Sally that followed?" and "What did you hope this line of inquiry would produce?"

Example 2: The Challenge

An employee believed that he was fired because of his age. The employer insisted that the termination was based on a broad, company-wide reduction in employment. In the mediation session, the employer was represented by the employee's previous supervisor. The mediator (an apprentice) began the mediation with a competent and thorough opening statement. He was interrupted by the employee, who said, "Have you ever been fired? If not, how could you possibly know what I am going through? How can you really help me?" The mediator responded, "Well, I've never been fired, that's true, but I really don't think that will make any difference." At that moment the mediator turned to the coach and asked for assistance.

> *Mediator:* I feel stumped. What do I do now?
> *Coach:* What is going on for you?
> *Mediator:* I feel challenged by the employee's question, like she is putting me on the spot.

The coach began by helping the mediator focus on an event that had caused concern and in this way demonstrated one aspect of the interactive process: heightened attention to the specific interactions that produced the particular question, surprise, or uncertainty. In this situation, the coach wanted to understand the mediator's experience, to know more about the sense of being stumped. The coach did not want to begin solving the problem until he knew more about it. He used an elicitive question to prompt the mediator to reflect on her experience. He was aware that the process of exploration and discovery is the heart of the learning opportunity.

> *Coach:* What made this seem like an effort to put you on the spot?
> *Mediator:* I became the issue, not the conflict between the parties.
> *Coach:* How did you become the issue?

The goal of coaching is to tap into the mediator's knowledge, believing that the mediator is capable of identifying the problem. Continuing to use questions that draw out information and reactions, the coach prompted the mediator to examine her role in the situation. To the extent that the mediator could identify and acknowledge the problem, she would be in a better position to find the solution. (For a poetic expression of the role of the teacher as a guide to one's own learning, see *The Prophet* [Gibran, 1995]*.)

> *Mediator:* My credibility and neutrality were called into
> question.
> *Coach:* Yes, but why was that so difficult for you to address?

The coach next guided the mediator to identify the source of the problem, namely, the mediator's reaction to the employee's question. Note that all of the coach's questions encouraged exploration and discovery. He did not introduce his own explanation for why the mediator reacted in such a puzzling and defensive manner.

> *Mediator:* Well, I was afraid that no matter what I said I was
> likely to upset one of the parties. So I felt stymied, and that
> made me feel as though I was the focus, not the parties.
> *Coach:* Whose issue is this?
> *Mediator:* It's the parties' issue.

In this exchange, the mediator came to understand her dilemma. To support the mediator's exploration of the problem, its origin, and its solution, the coach asked questions designed to help the mediator understand the nature and source of the problem. Using the principles and methods of reflective practice, the coach generated a possible explanation for the behavior (a working formulation), then

---

*We would like to thank Anne-Marie G. Hammond for providing the reference.

employed a series of elicitive questions to determine whether the formulation was accurate and complete. At the same time, the coach was teaching the mediator to employ these skills.

> *Coach:* So, what can you do to turn the issue back to the parties?
> *Mediator:* I can just ask the employee.

Note that the coach did not provide the answer but patiently worked with the mediator, who having clarified the nature of the problem could then develop a responsive and helpful approach.

Following this dialogue, the mediator continued the session, first asking the employee, "Tell me why it is important to you to know whether I've ever been fired?" The employee replied, "I want to be sure that you aren't going to take the employer's side in this mediation." The mediator turned to the employer and asked whether this was also a concern for her, and the employer indicated that it was not. Then the mediator said, "As I understand my role here, I am not taking sides; I am here to help the two of you talk about and find answers to your conflict. Is that agreeable?" The parties affirmed that it was, and the mediation continued.

During a subsequent debriefing, the following dialogue occurred:

> *Coach:* What was your experience the second time?
> *Mediator:* I was able to move off the issue of my having been
> fired and deal with the employee's question, seeing it as
> asking for information rather than as challenging my role.
> It seemed so easy; I realized that it was their issue, and the
> issue was defined as the mediator's neutrality, not the
> mediator.

As in the earlier exchange, the coach used an elicitive question to stimulate the mediator's reflective process.

> *Coach:* Why do you think you initially experienced the
> employee's question as a challenge?

Mediator: I'd never been challenged like that. I had no experience. So I felt I had to do something to persuade the employee that I wouldn't be biased against him, and then I realized that the employer might mistake that for bias, so I was stuck.

Coach: What helped you the second time, when you said it seemed so easy?

Mediator: Well, I saw that I was being defensive, and that made the issue mine, not the employee's. So, asking for clarification had the effect of acknowledging that the concern belonged to the employee, and it helped me stay neutral.

Throughout these conversations, the coach used questions only to encourage the mediator to reflect on and talk about the experience in the role-play. Although the coach might have had knowledge or expertise that could have been brought to bear in solving the mediator's dilemma, the coach resisted the chance to provide a solution. This coaching process emphasized the mediator's learning, his exploration and discovery.

At no time did the coach criticize the mediator or analyze the mediator's behavior or responses. At the heart of an elicitive approach is the absence of faultfinding or approval. Mediators can and will learn from their own experiences, and interpreting, judging, or even praising their efforts stifles efforts to uncover and make sense of the experience. Although in some instances it may be necessary to provide instruction or guidance (see the next example), such teaching approaches should be used sparingly.

The coach's goals for this learning opportunity were as follows:

- Encourage and assist the mediator in reflecting on his experience through a process of exploration and inquiry
- Support the mediator in discovering why the experience was surprising

- Engage the mediator in identifying new knowledge that can be used both in the current situation and in other situations
- Help the mediator learn the process and value of reflection

The coach modeled the reflective process and in this way taught the mediator how to engage in reflection on action.

Example 3: Two Neighbors

This example illustrates the joint use of both the elicitive and the prescriptive approach. The coach employed methods similar to those we have previously described and provided alternative intervention techniques that the mediator might employ when confronted with parties who frequently interrupt one another.

Two neighbors, Fran and Sal, were attempting to resolve a conflict that had arisen the previous week. It had so upset them that they were willing to put aside their mutual mistrust to seek a solution to their current problem. Fran's dog, Skippy, a favorite pet, roamed the neighborhood despite pleas from neighbors to keep the animal on a leash. Sal owned and boarded horses. Recently Skippy had gotten into the horse barn and bothered a newly boarded horse that kicked down the stall door, escaped into the paddock, and tried to jump the fence, causing a minor injury to its right foreleg. Sal saw Skippy chasing the horse and fired a shot to scare the animal. Skippy was only wounded; the horse's leg would heal.

The mediator (a novice) completed her opening statement and asked the parties to describe why they had come to a mediator. As Fran began to tell her story, interlacing criticism of Sal with her narrative of the events, Sal continually interrupted to correct Fran or to issue her own volley of accusations and denunciations. The mediator attempted to control this behavior by reminding the parties of their agreement to abide by certain ground rules, including their commitment not to interrupt one another. Despite the mediator's comments, the frequency of the interruptions increased, the parties became more aggressive, and their language became more caustic. The coach intervened.

> *Coach:* What's happening here?
> *Mediator:* They just want to fight. Neither of them is listening to me. It's getting much worse, not better.

Asking rather than telling is the key to the elicitive approach to coaching—in other words, helping the student identify the problem. Many coaches would use the prescriptive approach and begin with an instruction, offering the student an alternative technique that might move the parties away from the unproductive exchange of accusations and toward a more helpful presentation of their stories.

> *Coach:* What's happening for you as these two disputants continue to fight and interrupt?
> *Mediator:* I feel frustrated. I want them to stop their behavior, and they just won't listen to me.

To locate the explanations of the dilemma and to generate possible responses, the coach focused attention on the interactions among the parties and the mediator. He wanted to be sure that the mediator was aware of her own reactions to the continuing escalation of the conflict.

> *Coach:* What are you observing?
> *Mediator:* No matter what I try, they keep arguing and not listening to one another.
> *Coach:* How do you think you could be helpful to them?
> *Mediator:* I tried stopping them, reminding them of the ground rules, and that didn't seem to make any difference.
> *Coach:* Let me suggest a possible explanation for their behavior. Is it possible that they don't understand your role, and that they are trying to persuade you to take sides?

Mediator: That's possible, though I did tell them at the beginning that I was not a judge and wouldn't make any decisions. And they seemed to understand my role.

Sensing the mediator's frustration, the coach offered an alternative view of the parties' behavior—as a possibility, not as a conclusive explanation. This gave the mediator an opportunity to reflect on the idea and make her own assessment as to its relevance and usefulness.

Coach: Any other ideas why they are behaving this way?
Mediator: Well, maybe this is how they have argued in the past. Or maybe they're just really upset.

When she rejected the coach's possible explanation, the mediator was invited to develop alternatives. The coach was helping the mediator learn to problem solve for herself, to reflect on the experience, and to test out possible explanations until she arrived at a formulation that fit.

Coach: So, what could you do to test your explanations?
Mediator: I could remind them that this is a place where they can talk more constructively.
Coach: And what do you think would happen if you did that?
Mediator: I guess they'd just continue to fight.

The coach again used elicitive questions to stimulate the mediator's thinking, to encourage reflection, and to nurture the mediator's discovery of the limitations of her possible interventions.

Coach: So that's not going to work. When people are obviously upset, do you think that telling them to behave is likely to change their behavior? You need to get them to talk about what's bothering them, and to tell you why it's so difficult to be polite.

Mediator: So I could just ask them why they are interrupting? Or why they aren't listening to one another? And if I did so, then they would be thinking about whether they really wanted to be in mediation, and what they'd need to do to participate constructively.

At this moment, the coach was telling, or reminding, the student of a fundamental principle of human nature that affected her choice of intervention. This is an excellent example of the interlacing of prescriptive and elicitive modes of coaching—using questions, except in situations where presenting information would be more useful and appropriate.

Coach: That's right. Help them take responsibility, by engaging them, not by scolding them.

Mediator: I see now how I can approach them.

The coach reinforced the lesson: People respond more positively when invited to take a role in shaping their behavior than when told how they should behave. At the same time, the mediator learned alternative approaches, developing her capacity for analysis, critical thinking, and problem solving. She understood the need for an extensive repertoire of techniques, and learned an equally vital lesson, how to determine which technique to employ, when, and why.

These examples demonstrate how coaching supports the development of the abilities necessary for competent professional practice. This form of coaching also encourages mediators to learn and use the habits of reflective practice and interactive process that lead toward artistry. Coaching that relies on elicitive questions is grounded in a system of beliefs, encourages curiosity, and supports the exploration of the terrain of professional practice.

The Path to Artistry

In the poem, "The Road Not Taken," Robert Frost envisions a traveler on a journey through the woods facing a choice between two paths, one well-worn, the other less traveled. And like the traveler who chooses the latter, we follow the less worn path, the one we believe is more certain to lead to artistry.

We approach the task of assisting individuals along the path of professional development with the following beliefs:

- Each person has the ability to attain artistry, in some measure.
- The discipline and practices that lead to artistry are learnable.
- The manifestation of artistry is unique to each setting and to each person.
- Artistry may rely on inherent talents but it is gained only through discipline, intention, and practice.
- Artistry requires a thorough understanding of the traditions, principles, and practices of a profession.

Our coaching and our approach to mediator education in general are grounded in these beliefs. We guide, assist, support, and encourage our students to explore the terrain of professional practice. We do not see ourselves as experts in a model of practice in which we inculcate our students. We do not see the journey of professional development as an investigation, a search for an established set of principles and practices that define the profession. Instead, we encourage students to explore what is unknown as well as what is known. We want students to study and learn the traditions—the collection of practice skills and the body of knowledge that constitute the profession of mediation. In addition, however, we encourage our students to test the limits of that knowledge, to challenge current views, and to seek new applications of their skills and knowledge.

They will thus make discoveries about themselves, their clients, and their profession. These are the surprises of which Schön (1983, 1987) speaks—those unexpected, unusual events and experiences that challenge out current understanding of our work, test the limits of our knowledge, and call for innovation.

If professional development is a process of exploration, then we must support mediators in their inquiry. Too often, in the service of helping students learn what it means to be a professional, educators present a model of practice that limits curiosity and exploration. We must acknowledge that each student's journey along the path of knowledge is unique and will not follow a predictable path. Supporting students as they explore the less traveled path, as in the Robert Frost poem noted at the beginning of this section, encourages curiosity, develops a questioning mind, and ultimately leads to an enhanced capacity for critical thinking.

As teachers and coaches, we use an elicitive method—questions that assist the student on the learning journey and encourage independent thinking, personal exploration, and inventiveness. This approach alters the traditional relationship between student and teacher. In our view, teachers are not experts who impart knowledge, but guides who assist and escort students in their journey to acquire the skills and knowledge of a competent professional.

Teachers and coaches may also assert a more traditional role— imparting a body of knowledge or a set of practice skills. This is most explicitly demonstrated in the third example, where we see the coach presenting information to the mediator. At the same time, the mediator is encouraged to consider for herself the value of the proposed strategy. Imparting data does not interfere with the mediator's exploration; it helps provide information that can be used in the discovery process. The coach offers a map that illustrates many choices for the journey and invites the mediator to consider which of the routes will be most suitable. The mediator is encouraged to evaluate the data, not merely to accept and incorporate them. In this process, the student builds the skills of reflective practice and interactive process, the habits and disciplines that lead toward artistry.

Walking the Path of Artistry

Following your next mediation session, take time to think about what occurred and select one portion that seems significant for whatever reason. Write out the dialogue as best you can, in a form similar to one of the examples in this chapter. What did you say and what occurred in response? What did one of the participants say and how did you respond? Once you have completed the dialogue, then answer the following questions. If you have colleagues with whom you work or from whom you receive supervision, ask one of them to interview you.

- What was the significant moment in this portion of the session?
- Of all the interactions, why was this one important to you?
- What was happening for the participants?
- What was occurring for you?
- What did you observe that caught your attention?
- How were your interventions related to what you noticed?
- What do you think was the source of the participants' actions and reactions?

Upon completing this activity, note any new ideas or approaches that emerged. Also, reflect on the process itself, how asking these questions stimulated your ability to recall events and dialogue.

Looking Back, Looking Forward

Individuals will advance along the continuum of professional development when, in addition to receiving instruction in the fundamental skills and basic knowledge of the discipline, they also learn to apply the principles and methods of interactive process and reflective practice. The novice, apprentice, and practitioner become increasingly talented at utilizing a repertoire of skills and strategies in response to predictable behaviors and problem situations they have learned to identify. They will, however, reach a limit to their professional development unless they can master the hallmarks of artistry. Professionals may become sophisticated, resourceful, and ingenious in addressing the challenges of their practices. Despite these professional gains, artistry will remain elusive until they learn to apply the methods and principles of reflective practice and interactive process.

In the following sections we continue our examination of reflective practice and interactive process. We define the principles and methods that characterize each element, and we consider how they are useful to the practitioner in developing artistry.

Part Two

Reflective Practice

Chapter Four

Finding Your Formulation

The first part of this book describes how the two processes of reflective practice and interactive process can fuse into artistry in professional practice. The second part of the book is entirely about the nature and use of reflection. In this chapter and the next, we further describe the two objects on which an artistic mediator reflects: the *formulation*, or an explanation for the conflict and the parties' responses; and the theoretical and informational base that guides practitioners—the mediator's *constellation of* theories. In Chapter Six, the final chapter in this section, we further describe the way in which the reflective process functions when it is being used to serve the goal of artistry.

A formulation is a mediator's conceptualization of a case, a complex, integrated way of making sense out of the experiences, behaviors, and conversations of the mediation session. When done well, a formulation is a comprehensive set of ideas that explain to the mediator what is going on in a particular case (see Figure 4.1). It is unique and specific to the case, and like a special recipe or the formula for a product, it is made up of components that create something when they are put together. It is composed of at least three parts: (1) the characteristics of the disputants, (2) the context and type of dispute, and (3) the methodology of mediation that would be the most helpful in working out the particular type of dispute with the type of people involved.

A formulation is created by the mediator very early in the mediation and is evolutionary. The development of a formulation begins with basic information about the dispute and the participants,

Figure 4.1. The Formulation.

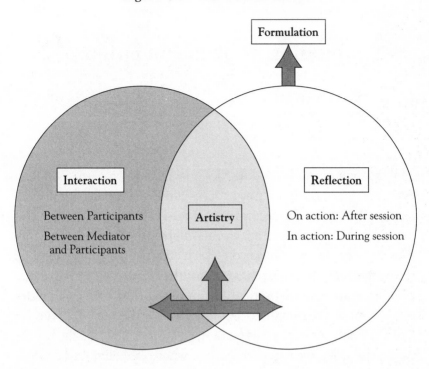

on the basis of which the mediator makes some initial and cursory assumptions about why the participants are in dispute, about the nature and source of their conflict, and about the types of interventions that are likely to be helpful. An initial formulation, based on such limited information, is understandably indefinite and fluid. To develop a formulation at this beginning stage in the process, a mediator must use intuition and hunches. Until he or she can secure enough information to determine what is happening with the people and the dispute and then have some ideas about what methods might work best, the formulation may be very thin and unspecific. This initial formulation will undergo revision as the mediator gains additional information about the dispute, observes the parties' interactions, and reflects on their responses to interventions. The mediator's goal, as described in Hallmark 4 in Chapter Two, is to hold on tightly and let go lightly—to be intentional about developing formulations without becoming so attached to them as to ignore signs that they are not accurate or complete.

A formulation could also be called a *working hypothesis* in that it is speculative until fully developed. Like a hypothesis, it is an intelligent guess or hunch that will be either confirmed or changed depending on the information gathered by the mediator. We have adopted the term *formulation* rather than *hypothesis* because hypotheses are usually proved true or false whereas a formulation does not respond to and need not be bound by this dichotomy. It represents less of a reductionist, either-or orientation than a this-plus-this-plus-this, additive synthesis.

In every mediation situation, mediators make formulations about the case that include, at a minimum, the mediator's current understandings of the people, the context of the dispute, and the types of interventions and the mediation process the mediator is likely to employ. The formulation may also take into account the legal context of the case, as part of the mediator's understanding about the parties' level of motivation to mediate and about the type of dispute in which they are involved. A complete and helpful formulation often also includes ideas about the underlying conflicts, the power dynamics, the immediacy of the need for resolution, the types of conflicts involved (structural, data, relationship, value, and interest), and the interventions and models that might be most effective.

Defining a Formulation

Mediators make a formulation quickly and most often unconsciously and begin to act out of that formulation during the early stages of the mediation. A formulation that is well considered and thoughtfully constructed is powerful, because it connects theory and action. Whether acknowledged explicitly or functioning implicitly, the mediator's principles, beliefs, knowledge, and values (constellation of theories) operate as the filter through which the mediator sifts information and observations in order to develop a formulation. Whether operating with an acknowledged or an unexpressed theoretical framework, the mediator makes decisions and implements strategies on the basis of the formulation. The mediator's constellation of theories, the grounding principles on which practice decisions are based, is like a lens that regulates the mediator's vision of the conflict situation and the parties. A formulation is created by the context of the mediator's constellation of theory but can also reshape that constellation of theory through reflection. This is why a reflective practitioner who aims for artistry must understand the basis for a formulation. Formulations that are created consciously and deliberately guide and inform the mediator's work.

The following three examples illustrate how the formulation of a case is based on a mediator's understanding of three intersecting factors: the people, the dispute, and the preferred mediation process.

1. The mediator in a divorce case started routinely going through his usual protocol of describing the nature of mediation, the role of the mediator, and the limits of confidentiality. At that point one disputant interrupted and blurted out, "I have schizo-affective disorder and my doctor says I can think just fine and I am fine to go through mediation, but I can't keep the house clean like my husband wants so I want you to help him see that I am fine and that I can live on my own."

The mediator's initial formulation had been that these were people in situational distress caused by the stress of separation and a pending divorce and that the conventional mediation process and techniques would be appropriate. However, new information about one party's mental illness challenged that initial formulation. Learning this, the mediator was then obligated to evaluate whether the initial formulation was accurate and complete, or whether it should be revised. The client was trying, albeit rather crudely, to let the mediator know that she had special needs and that the mediator should take time to learn about them. The mediator needed to change the initial formulation based on this new input, to reformulate the case, acknowledging that the client was a person with long-term mental health issues who may need the mediator to make special adjustments in pace and method in order to serve her needs better.

2. In a dispute brought to a community mediation center, the mediator's initial formulation indicated that the dispute involved both the location of a basketball hoop and also who would bear responsibility for the damage to a neighbor's flowers caused by the kids who used the hoop. That was how the disputants had framed the dispute. After some discussion it became apparent that the dispute was more complex, involving neighbors who had a negative history with each other. Because damage to the flowers was minimal, the dispute seemed to be constructed out of a series of overreactions. The mediator learned, upon further exploration, that the real concern of one neighbor was whether the other neighbor was racially biased. The hoop had been in place for three years without incident, and the only new factor was that some children who did not live on the street and who were of a different ethnicity than the residents of the area had recently used the hoop. On the basis of this information, the mediator changed the initial formulation to include not only the manifest conflict about the placement of the basketball hoop and damage to the flowers but also the question of whether the underlying conflict involved one neighbor's longstanding personal prejudice, which may or may not be mediable.

3. In a mediation dealing with a parent-teen conflict that involved issues of dating and curfew, the mediator developed an initial formulation that the dispute involved the adolescent's efforts to exert some control over decisions affecting her life, while her parents were unwilling to relinquish their power over her. The teenager gave emotionally flat responses to the mediator's questions, which might indicate resistance to mediation or might mean reluctance to talk about what was troubling her. The mediator sensed that something more serious might be involved. Although the preferred approach in this mediation program was to stay in joint session as much as possible, the mediator decided to hold a brief caucus with

each party, starting with the teen. During the private session the teen revealed a long history of neglectful and questionable parenting and reported a recent event in which physical violence had erupted in the home, first between the mother and the teen, then including the stepfather, who hit the teen hard enough to leave bruises. The domestic violence and the teen's fear of harm had gone unreported to anyone until now. This unexpected revelation had a significant impact on the mediator's formulation and subsequent approach to the dispute and the parties. Suddenly, the mediator's formulation about the people changed, as did the formulation about the nature of the dispute.

Initial formulations are by definition thin and based on limited information, yet mediators have to start with some notion about the parties and the dispute. As the interactions continue during the session, the mediator takes into consideration any additional information that becomes available and changes the formulation to match the experience and perceptions of the parties. An initial formulation, made in the first five minutes, will undoubtedly change by the end of a session. A formulation that cannot grow and change becomes stunted, rigid, and unhelpful and can actually lead the mediator in the wrong direction in dealing with the dispute and the parties.

Thick, rich, and pliable formulations can include a range of factors and interactions unique to the case. Developing and modifying formulations is part of the conflict assessment that some writers suggest is a necessary part of the mediation process (Folberg and Taylor, 1984; Wilmot and Hocker, 1998). If the assessment is thorough and complete, the expanded formulation will have greater substance, and thus enhanced value. The more expanded the formulation is, the more it will help the mediator make meaning and sense out of the parties' experiences and out of the interactions during the mediation. The following questions can be used in creating an initial formulation and in continuing to reflect on this formulation to see if it must change:

Characteristics of the Disputants

- Are the disputants in crisis as well as in conflict?
- What is their motivation in terms of the dispute and in terms of their participation in mediation?
- What are their positions and interests?
- What is their range of flexibility with regard to exploring options for resolution?
- Are there other complicating factors (such as limited time or money; drugs or alcohol abuse; mental or emotional health issues; control, abuse, and violence issues; language or cultural factors)?
- Do they understand their own sources of power?
- What outside forces are influencing the parties (such as attorneys, unions, advocates, family members, therapists, or friends)?

Characteristics of the Dispute

- What types of conflict (relationship, data, structural, values, or interest) are involved in this dispute?
- What is the presenting (manifest) conflict? Are there underlying conflicts?
- At what stage of dispute resolution have you entered the mediation (prefiling, a state of uncertainty, or preparing for litigation)?
- What have been the trigger events?
- What are the external power dynamics that the disputants face?
- What are the legal issues inherent in the dispute?

The Methodology for Mediation

- Are the parties ready for mediation?
- What other services do they need before, concurrently with, or after the mediation?

- What special accommodations or adaptations to the usual mediation process (such as phones, extensive use of private sessions, or special rules) might be required?
- Are there other parties (secondary stakeholders, such as children, supervisors, or new partners) who might be affected by the outcome, and do they need to be included in some way in the mediation process?

A formulation is like a road map that helps the mediator make meaning and sense out of the information generated through mediation and of the parties' interactions. The mediator uses the formulation to guide the journey of the mediation, to select routes, and to help make decisions when there are forks in the road. Like travelers, mediators tend to follow paths they have previously walked; they use methods with which they are familiar. They may make choices about direction, speed, and path without much deliberation, resorting to the well known, customary routes. We encourage mediators to be thoughtful and deliberate about these plans, to identify and then explore the assumptions that inform their decisions, to use reflective process to generate and test ideas and formulations. In doing so, mediators will advance along the path to artistry. Unfortunately, mediators too often fail to articulate and make explicit their formulations as they proceed with a case or refuse to change it based on new information. They operate out of a formulation without being aware of how it shapes their practice. To bring artistry to their practice, mediators need to uncover, articulate, and test their formulations.

Formulations Are Dependent on Theory

Obviously, to develop an initial or evolving formulation, mediators refer back to their own constellation of theories that inform them about people, about conflict situations, and about the mediator's role. These beliefs, values, principles, and theoretical concepts act as the lenses through which mediators view the data gained in a mediation. Formulations have as much to do with the mediator's constellation of theories as with the information gathered during the mediation session. For example, in a divorce mediation, mediators usually have some sense of whether stressed and edgy disputants are experiencing situational stress due to the divorce or whether preexisting mental health issues are compounding the usual divorce issues.

Mediators trained as mental health professionals might include information about each person's mental health status in their initial formulations. Regardless of their professional training, many mediators do not want to diagnose their clients—that is, they do not want to use a medical model of diagnosis, prognosis, or treatment. Other mediators observe possible mental health issues but lack relevant theory and training. And a mediator who knows a lot of theory about early childhood development might formulate a visitation dispute case differently than a mediator who has a very thick and rich negotiation theory but little knowledge of the age-related stages that children experience.

Lack of a theory base can lead to an incomplete or inaccurate formulation. For example, mediators who hold beliefs about the efficacy of problem solving but lack clinical theory may develop rich and useful formulations that are built around those concepts but may miss subtle hints of depression or resistance. Similarly, mediators who do not understand the issues and patterns of domestic violence and intimidation may miss signs of one party's efforts to exert power and control over the other.

What matters is not so much the specific formulation created by the mediator but that the mediator has created a formulation that takes into account key information from the parties, that it is grounded in relevant theory, and that it explains and makes sense of the parties and their dispute. On the basis of this formulation the mediator builds interventions and interactions with the disputants. Mediators' strategies and interventions are directly related to how they think about and formulate a case because all people act on what they think. When they ground their formulations in solid models and theories, their formulations are strong and accurate. When clear and sound formulations guide the mediator's actions and decisions, they lead to effective, competent, and potentially artful practice.

Why and How a Formulation Changes

Because a formulation is experimental, it is changeable. Mediators develop then continually test their formulations, deciding whether they are suitable and fit the situation and the parties. Sometimes what is workable at the outset of a mediation needs to change. Mediators start with either a conscious or unconscious formulation that seems appropriate to the circumstances of the dispute, but that formulation needs to be examined, reflected on, and tested throughout the mediation. To do this requires a beginner's mind—one that is supple and flexible, curious, and open to new ideas. Mediators can evolve their thinking about a case only if they are receptive to fresh ideas and new perspectives during interactions and are also willing to reflect on the formulation. As we note in Chapter Six, the first task of reflective practitioners is to reflect in action on their initial formulations and continually engage in such reflection throughout the mediation.

For example, in the mediation of a workplace conflict between coworkers, if the mediator formulates that the problem in the office stems from one party's attitude toward his coworkers, that formulation may lead to an emphasis on the individual's relationship with the members of his work group. If the mediator's constellation of theories includes concepts such as Moore's (1996), in which a single dispute may embody multiple causes of conflict, the formulation might emphasize not only the worker's attitude but also the structural conditions involved in the workplace itself. Mediators who have read and understood attribution theory, who have been exposed to social constructionist theories, or who are well-versed in the concepts of systems theory might construct a very different formulation by including concepts from those theories. The next chapter deals extensively with identifying, locating, and understanding one's unique theory base. It is important here to understand that mediators' theories will influence their ability to create and use a formulation to best advantage.

Ideally formulations change as a result of the mediator's attention to interactions in the sessions, and also through reflection during and after sessions. When mediators hold on to formulations that are incomplete or that do not adequately and accurately explain what is going on, they may feel confused, and this confusion sets up conditions that can lead to inconsistencies, negative process dynamics, and even power struggles. Sometimes mediators are totally oblivious to how discrepant their formulations are when compared to the reality of the interaction in front of them. When mediators cannot see how far off the mark their formulations are, they lack the insight to change them. Constant reflection helps to ensure that formulations are accurate, well grounded, and complete.

One way in which mediators try to deal with the gap between an incorrect or incomplete formulation and the reality of a dispute is by insisting that the disputants follow the mediator's formulation rather than by shifting the formulation to match the parties' experience. This behavior leads to poor interaction and rapport, and in the worst case, to unnecessary dissatisfaction with the mediation process. The formulation should be changeable, permeable, and fluid so that mediators will match their concepts to reality rather than the other way around. If mediators gather enough facts and material each session, if they carefully observe the parties' interactions, and if they then use the information gathered to recast their formulations, the direction, flow, and structure of the mediation process will necessarily be affected. Mediators not only must reflect on their current formulations but also must learn from their efforts and incorporate these lessons into their constellation of theories.

For example, a party in a divorce mediation announced that she was deathly afraid of her former marital partner and that he was outside the building, waiting to get her. She looked panic-stricken, was making frantic calls to several places on her cellular phone, and was unable to follow much of what the mediator was saying. The mediator calmly walked her back to his office, away from view of the street, and sat calmly with her for about ten minutes while encouraging her to tell him more about the history of the encounters that had made her so afraid.

The mediator's initial formulation of this case included the following:

- The woman was a victim of prolonged domestic violence who needed further protection.

- The case might not be mediable because of this concern for safety.

- As a case involving domestic violence, the mediation (if convened) might require accommodations to the usual process, such as special rules about who comes and goes first, use of telephone mediation instead of in-person sessions, or requiring the victim to have a safety plan and restraining order in place before going any further.

As the woman continued talking, her anxiety ceased and she told a very complex story. The mediator learned that the state's Children's Protective Services had intervened, taking the children out of the woman's care and putting them in temporary custody of the father, and that a temporary custodial order was still in place. It also turned out that the woman's last attempt to renew an old restraining order against her former husband had been denied by a judge, based on lack of evidence of threat of harm.

Suddenly the mediator's formulation changed. Instead of seeing the woman as a person swept up in the situational distress of divorce, the mediator realized that the woman was not a helpless victim but rather someone with a potential mental health condition that made her inordinately suspicious of her former husband's motives. The mediator still questioned the mediability of the case, but for a different set of reasons—namely, the active involvement of Children's Protective Services and the possibility of past, current, or future child abuse.

The woman's tears suddenly stopped. She grabbed a pen to map out for the mediator the complex situation she faced, including her ex-husband's recent action before the court to change the custody permanently to him. More of the family history and of the woman's current predicament had come to light, requiring a different formulation. But seeing only one person in the family system limited the mediator's ability to ensure that that formulation would be reasonably accurate and reliable.

At this point, the mediator had two parallel and equally useful but disparate formulations that could explain and make meaning out of the woman's story. To choose a course of action, the mediator needed to reflect on these formulations and select one. In the first formulation, the intimidation felt by the wife was real and was a manipulative maneuver on the part of the former husband to maintain power and control. In the second, equally plausible formulation, the man was not actively terrorizing his former wife but instead was desperately trying to secure his children from an abusive mother who was acting out and having difficulty emotionally. In the first view, the woman was honestly scared by an intimidating former spouse who was using a manipulative strategy to gain custody while discrediting the woman as mentally unstable. In the second view, the woman was probably not able to mediate, for mental and emotional reasons. According to the first view, the case was mediable, with some adaptations of process; according to the second view, it was not mediable at all.

Both formulations were incomplete and inconclusive. To select between these two incompatible formulations of the people, the problem, and the process, the mediator needed more information about the parties and their dispute. He would have to test out these two formulations. He would have to experiment in order to learn whether the former husband would voluntarily participate in mediation, to verify the extent of involvement of the state's Children's Protective Services, and to determine whether the case was mediable.

The mediator continued to reflect on the information and created yet another formulation. In this view, the woman was compromised in her parenting not through manipulation or intimidation by her former husband through domestic violence but through her own abusive actions toward the children. If this were true, the case could not be mediated for custody because Protective Services would decide who would have custody.

By using this reflective process, the mediator noticed that his view of the case had changed entirely. Instead of viewing it as a "he said, she said" dichotomy of who was "bad," the mediator reflected on the entire situation and discovered that looking at the problem rather than at the people was a more useful way of formulating the case. What might be mediable was the woman's parenting time, taking into account her history of either inadequate or abusive parenting and her current mental and emotional status. Moreover, if the parties could participate in a mediation, if there were issues that could be mediated, it was not clear whether accommodations needed to be made because of possible domestic violence and whether it would be prudent or appropriate to bring these two people together. By thinking differently, by formulating the case around what was potentially mediable, including methods that might protect the parties, the mediator's formulation shifted and expanded. He incorporated what was known into the formulation and then used experimentation to make new discoveries that led to subsequent changes in the formulation.

Using Formulations for Experimentation

As recently as twenty years ago, in professional counseling schools counselors were urged to choose one base model, such as the Rogerian approach or Ellis's rational-emotive model of counseling, and adhere strictly to its tenets, out of fear that creeping eclecticism might render that counselor less effective. In this book, we argue for a form of enlightened eclecticism for mediators, which requires mediators not to borrow a little from this and little from that but rather to have multiple responses for diverse conditions. Because formulations have multiple factors and can change, they become de facto eclectic.

The toolbox analogy is appropriate here. If you have multiple tools but do not understand why you should use a wrench for a particular job rather than a screwdriver, you may well select a wrench and do a good job but you will not understand what tool to use the next time. You will in effect be a skilled technician but have no understanding or ability to adapt. If you use a wrench really well but cannot explain why you selected that tool and what uses to make of it, your skill at using the wrench will have limited application.

Mediators should be experimenters. By maintaining a spirit of curiosity and being open to exploration, mediators not only reflect on the experiences of the mediation but also invite the disputants (through experimentation) to help them understand the conflict and the parties' perspectives. In this way mediators learn to make sense of the conflict and thereby create a more accurate and helpful formulation. To experiment, mediators may ask the disputants to confirm a certain view about the conflict and the parties, or they may ask the disputants to help them understand the reality of the disputants' experiences. Mediators may also share their formulations with disputants, to learn whether they are accurate, complete, and useful. Because mediators rely on theory to develop formulations, the richer and more extensive their foundation in theory is, the more they can experiment to determine how well the formulation fits the parties and their dispute.

The experimentation we recommend is not a crude trial-and-error process. Rather, it provides opportunities to test assumptions, to evaluate formulations, by utilizing what is known to uncover what is not known. Experimentation is not exploitive, nor does it involve the mediator playing or toying with the clients. What we mean by experimentation is the notion that mediators should be flexible in developing and testing their formulations; they should remain open to new information. As noted in Chapter Three, mediators who enact a reflective approach must not only experiment;

they must also suspend judgment and question assumptions. By remaining curious and willing to explore unknown terrain, they engage in a process that is necessary to test, evaluate, and recreate formulations.

Barriers to Awareness

There are several reasons why mediators might not be open to understanding their own formulations. First, mediators can be so scripted in their approach to mediation that they cannot see what is unique about each case. Once, in a training session, a mediator of some eminence agreed to mediate a simulated conflict situation. The quality of the mediator's effort was shockingly and surprisingly poor. As we engaged the mediator in reflectively exploring his formulation, he was clearly unable to describe his sense of the dispute—how he saw the people, the conflict, and the methods and strategies he might utilize. When asked how his view of the dispute shaped his interventions, he grew defensive, saying, "I've been mediating for fifteen years and this is the way I have always done it." In essence, though he had mediated hundreds of cases, in fifteen years he had made only one formulation. He was unwilling to explore other possible interpretations of the conflict, and uninterested in discovering the basis for his formulation and in learning whether that formulation fit the dispute. He was locked into a rigid formulation that did not allow for variation or uniqueness. Whenever he dealt with a conflict involving issues similar to those in the simulation, he responded in exactly the same manner, uninterested in nuances or in characteristics that might be different or unique.

A second reason that mediators might be oblivious to or unaware of their formulations is that by their very nature, formulations are personal and revealing. Mediators' unique constellations of theories serve as lenses for examining conflict situations, and formulations are developed through the utilization of these lenses.

Some mediators in private practice believe they must maintain the role of expert, providing services that are perceived as unique. In a competitive market, a mediator might well try to hide trade secrets, or even try to copyright, patent, or trademark them, as inventors of other special formulations do. If a mediator becomes possessive and proprietary, if she cannot share a formulation of a case with other mediators, then that mediator will be following a script that has not been exposed to critical assessment. Keeping a formulation private may seem like a way to maintain expertise, but it ultimately will not foster the development of personal artistry. Guarding formulations is not helpful to growth as a practitioner, nor to the development of the field. Sharing formulations, exploring various ways of viewing conflict situations, enhances competence.

A third barrier to understanding and using a formulation is the fear a mediator feels when a formulation is not working or when the mediator cannot seem to understand what is happening in the mediation. This fear can produce a great deal of confusion, anxiety, and negativity. There is a level of vulnerability and risk involved in exposing our working assumptions and case formulations to others. Fear of failure, negative self-judgments, and concerns about competency can be barriers to mediators even when creating and articulating a formulation for themselves, let alone when sharing it with others. To become artistic, and thus more effective, mediators must create, become aware of, and share their formulations, and suspend the demands of ego that require perfection and complete understanding.

Problems with Formulations

Despite the usefulness of a clear and coherent formulation, there is an inherent concern that it might be used inappropriately, that it might not become a fluid, constantly changing set of concepts but instead become rigid and unchanging, that curiosity and exploration would be ignored. If a formulation were used to dominate a session, the mediator would be using it not to enhance the understanding and work of the session but rather to hide from what is really going on. Instead of illuminating the situation, the formulation would dominate, and instead of allowing meaning to emerge, the formulation would restrict the interaction. Instead of helping the mediator see what is happening, a formulation that cannot be questioned blocks awareness. Although the formulation is a reflection of the meaning and truth perceived by the mediator, it is imperative that the mediator realize that it is not *the* truth. In the chapters in Part Three of this book we discuss further how the formulation must respond to the interactive process of the mediation session itself.

Because a formulation acts like a filter of experience, it can become an imposition of the mediator's view on the participants. For example, if the mediator has assessed the parties as somehow damaged or incapable, as operating from a condition of low self-esteem, or as experiencing loss of power or learned helplessness, those perceptions may limit the mediator's ability to acknowledge and respond to information that conflicts with the assessment. If a mediator has determined that the parties are engaging in bad-faith negotiation, she may operate on the basis of this formulation for the rest of the session, oblivious to any cues that the disputants are in fact operating from a position of good faith. Formulations can so easily become a judgment of the parties or the dispute, or a set of inaccurate perceptions that block true understanding and artistic process. A formulation held inflexibly cannot grow and change as the session unfolds, and can lead to lowered rather than enhanced performance by the mediator. In the worst case, an untested and rigidly held formulation can result in the mediator insisting that the disputants act consistently with the mediator's formulation rather than the mediator adjusting the formulation to match the true interactions of the parties.

Rigid formulations can block the mediator's awareness of the disputants' true abilities or the true nature of the dispute, or they may constrain the mediator from using the most appropriate strategies and methods. For example, a formulation that a woman in a postdivorce dispute is unusually passive, perhaps a victim in the dispute, might lead to a strategy to even the playing field. In doing so, the mediator may actually create an unbalanced situation by inappropriately advocating for one party.

Properly constructed, formulations should not result in judgments about or labeling of participants. Formulations are not a cause for mediators to impose their beliefs and values on disputants; they should be a method by which mediators explore, gather, and give meaning to information about the conflict and the parties. Incomplete, inaccurate, or rigid formulations can harm the mediation process; a safeguard is the judicious use of reflective supervision to help mediators question the basis for and validity of their formulations and learn to use them more effectively. The perspective gained in supervision helps mediators understand how their formulations are developed and utilized; when their formulations have become unhelpful, rigid, and inflexible; and the process of altering their formulations.

Sharing Formulations with Clients

If formulations help mediators make sense and meaning out of the circumstances of the dispute and the parties' responses, is there purpose and value in sharing that understanding with the disputants? In artistic practice and during positive interaction that requires transparent practice, the mediator's formulation should not be a secret from the disputants. By sharing their formulations with disputants, mediators are able to test their validity and usefulness, to determine their accuracy and completeness, and to gain new information that may lead to recasting them. For example, by openly discussing a formulation that the difficulty in reaching agreement in a dispute over economic matters is in part the result of one disputant being more facile in negotiation than the other, the parties might respond by acknowledging the validity of the formulation, leading to interventions by the mediator that assist the parties' negotiations. In contrast, the mediator might learn that the block to a successful negotiation is lack of trust between the disputants that leads to their reluctance to engage in candid discussions. In response to this information, the mediator could adjust the formulation and design strategies and interventions that are more appropriate to the parties' understanding of the dispute.

Openly talking about their formulations may help mediators develop rapport with the disputants, build their trust in the mediation process, and gain their support for and cooperation in implementing certain strategies. If mediators believe in and value openness in their communications with disputants, they will actively encourage the disputants' participation in identifying and evaluating the formulations. Sharing case formulations with disputants can lead to greater attentiveness and increased cooperation from the disputants, and result in formulations that are relevant, helpful, and instrumental.

Writing Formulations

To increase artistry in your mediation practices, practice writing formulations of your cases at the end of the first session. This will serve as your initial formulation, which will be either supported or called into question as you continue to work with the disputants. By making the formulation explicit, you can identify your theoretical basis, note what you are overlooking, register your assumptions, discover what additional information you want to gather, and design experiments to test your formulation.

To quickly analyze the elements of a case, go back to the set of questions about people, problems, and process listed earlier in this chapter. Answering these questions for each case or session can serve as a guide for writing a formulation. If you use the same format from case to case, you will see trends emerging in your practice, and you will learn more about the method and factors you use in developing formulations. By engaging in this reflective process, you will become aware of your assumptions, the working principles that influence your formulations. By making explicit what is ordinarily implicit—by articulating your theories, beliefs, and values—you will become familiar with your method for developing formulations. You will enhance your capacity to make effective use of formulations in your practice.

Using Reflective Supervision to Shape Formulations

Formulations can change not only by virtue of insights gained through self-reflection but also by engaging in appropriate and frequent reflective supervision. Reflective supervisors help practitioners deconstruct their formulations. Because supervisors can have a more objective view of mediators' formulations, they can sometimes ask questions that help mediators identify the basis for their formulations, and over time the patterns and themes in the mediators' work will become visible. With this awareness, mediators can confirm or reshape their formulations. Reflective supervisors are not judgmental, second-guessing mediators' every decision; nor are they authority figures monitoring mediators' actions. The goals of reflective supervision, presented in greater detail in Chapter Six, are to help mediators identify their constellations of theories, discover their methods for developing formulations, uncover the assumptions that inform their work, and learn to be self-reflective.

In our work with graduate-level conflict resolution students, professionals coming back for retraining, and practicing mediators, we have found that the external supervisor not only acts as a coach, supporting and giving specific instructions for interventions, but can also help mediators learn about their constellations of theories. They are less involved in quality control and more engaged in research and development.

By utilizing their experience and their understanding of the mediation process, reflective supervisors guide the reflective process, nurture curiosity, help overcome resistance to new ideas, and encourage development of artistic practice.

Walking the Path of Artistry

At the end of your next mediation session, take twenty minutes to reflect on your formulation of the case. Use the set of questions suggested earlier in the chapter as a format for asking yourself about the characteristics of the case, about the starting assumptions and views you have about the parties, and about where in the conflict cycle the parties entered into mediation. Also list your reactions to the case: Are you angry at the people? Do you feel they are unreasonable? Are you feeling positive about the session? Then write out your formulation, as though you were preparing for another mediator to take over as of the next session. Be sure to analyze all aspects of the case, and explain to a colleague or supervisor the basis for your strategies and interventions—why you are doing what you are doing, and what connections you make between your actions and how the parties are responding.

Then assume the role of the incoming mediator. Question all assumptions. See if you can get a fuller picture. Then, as the next mediator, imagine you are presenting the case to other, novice mediators and explain what the case is all about. Actually sound pontifical if you must, but try to give the novices the benefit of your expertise in understanding all of the dimensions of the case.

Then imagine yourself as one of the novice mediators, who in response to your explanation asks, Why?—not to challenge authority but to understand and learn from this case lessons that might apply to future cases. See if in this role of learner you can get more information or understanding about the way the first mediator has made sense of the events and circumstances of the case.

Now return to your original role and see if any of the information you have obtained has been helpful in understanding what you really think about the people, the case, and the mediation process.

Looking Back, Looking Forward

Understanding the assumptions, impressions, and observations that have gone into your formulation of the disputants, the case, and the most effective methods for intervening helps mediators during a session. The formulation summarizes the ideas and thoughts that guide mediators' interactions—the ways in which they have made meaning for themselves of what is going on. Because all mediators create and rely on formulations, awareness of the basis for and use of a formulation in one case enhances mediators' capacity to utilize formulations in other mediation settings. In addition, by reflecting on formulations, mediators become aware of consistent patterns or trends that may enhance or limit their practices.

Finding, naming, and utilizing a formulation during a session, sharing it with the clients to ask for corroboration, and remaining open to experimentation and change based on the interactions in a session are part of the concept of reflection in action described more fully in Chapter Six. Becoming aware of what they know and questioning their formulations about the people, the conflict, and the best ways to mediate advance mediators along the path to artistry.

In the next chapter we will look at how formulations about a specific case are derived from the mediator's ongoing beliefs, abstract concepts and theoretical understanding, models of practice, and factual information. Together, these elements become the mediator's constellation of theories.

Chapter Five

Mapping Your Constellation of Theories

A mediator's constellation of theories provides a way to integrate what has already been learned with the current events and situations. This constellation of theories is used all the time to interpret and predict people's behavior and interactions, but it can be especially useful during mediation. It is our premise that all mediators have a constellation of theories that guides and informs their practice, whether they are aware of it or not.

Mediators who make use of the methods and principles of reflective practice are conscious of the unique set of facts, models of mediation, and core theories and values they bring to their practices. Mediators, as individuals, have been shaped by social learning and life experiences, and they have also been shaped by their profession and its unique blend of ideas and beliefs. They experience the world through the tinted lenses of their knowledge and experience. Those who want to make their mediation practice more artistic must reflect on and come to know fully what they know—their accumulated personal knowledge and understanding, which includes facts, models, theories, and core beliefs—their constellation of theories.

A constellation of theories is the sum of all the mediator knows, regardless of how that knowledge was acquired. Unlike a formulation, which is specific to only one conflict situation and its disputants, a constellation of theories is a vast, generalized store of information that shapes the mediator's understanding of people and experiences. Like a constellation of stars, a constellation of theories is large and expanding, yet somehow remote, mostly uncharted, and difficult to describe.

Unfortunately, few mediators take the time to map out their constellation of theories, to identify the thoughts, beliefs, values, and principles that are the foundation for the way they experience and understand behavior, events, and interactions. Failure to do so can lead to blind spots, which limit mediators' ability to understand, interpret, and act integratively. When mediators know their constellation of theories and understand how it guides and informs their work, they are better able to integrate this knowledge during a session, and this integration of theory with practice contributes to their artistry.

A constellation of theories is like a set of concentric circles (see Figure 5.1); each is a part of the whole, and each has different levels of organization and integration. They all work together synergistically, yet each level or ring has a different character. The outer rings of the constellation, the necessary facts and information that mediators use, are not less important than the inner rings; they are just somewhat less integrated with or more loosely connected to the central beliefs, values, and theories. The presence or absence of facts and information are not as central to the operation of the constellation as what is at the core.

A mediator's constellation of theories usually includes ideas and knowledge about such concepts as the nature of mankind and the nature of aggression, restorative justice, models of and approaches to mediation, the ethics of practice, and laws and other factors that are relevant to their work. Mediators who have not reflected on and attempted to understand this universe of the mind apply their beliefs and theories oblivious to how the structures within their constellation of theories direct their actions. Those who understand and can access their constellation of theories both when developing case formulations and when engaging with the disputants achieve informed, aware, and artistic responses to the parties and their conflicts. Like a formulation, a mediator's constellation of theories is what a reflective

Figure 5.1. The Constellation of Theories.

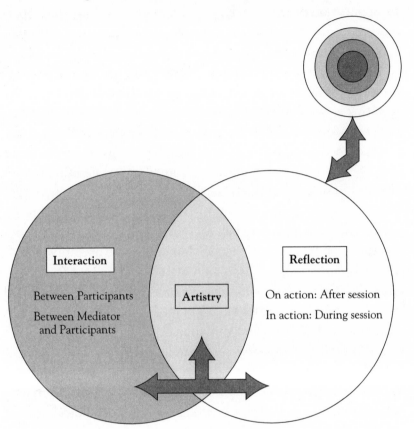

practitioner reflects on both during and after a session in order to attain artistry.

One way to think about a constellation of theories is to use a computer analogy. Using a certain model of mediation practice in mediation is like using a specific application program, such as WordPerfect, Eudora, Excel, or Lotus. The application program performs specific tasks. In some cases, competing models, such as Netscape and Explorer, may perform essentially the same functions. Similarly, mediators may adopt a model of mediation, such as those labeled transformative, structured, therapeutic, problem-solving, or interest-based negotiation, to guide and inform their work. Just as the application program is only one element of a computer's operations, so is the mediator's model only part of his or her constellation of theories.

These application programs, or models of mediation, are supported by what we do not readily see—in the computer it is the operating system, and for the mediator it is the facts, base theories, and core values and beliefs. Using the computer analogy, if the model of mediation is like an application program, then the other parts of the constellation of theories are like the operating system that runs the computer (such as DOS or OS-2), which supports and allows the application program to function. Like the an operating system, the mediator's core beliefs, values, and theories support the enactment of the mediation model. Just as the base operating system on a computer forms the basic architecture and support for the applications, the mediator's core theories and values provide the basic architecture and support for models of mediation. The operating system determines how the program runs. A mediator's core principles in the constellation of theories determine whether and how a model of mediation functions. These deeper theories and understandings, like the operating system, are less visible than the application program or model. The traces of their impact are discernable, but their codes cannot be as easily observed.

If the operating system of a computer malfunctions or is not compatible with the application program, the computer will not function properly or at all. If there are internal inconsistencies or incompatibilities within the theories that make up the constellation, the mediator will not be able to work effectively and may experience the behavioral equivalent of a computer glitch, endless loop, or frozen screen. If mediators lack an adequate theory to support their model of mediation, or if they do not understand the methods implicit in their model, they may apply the model ineffectively. A mediator who follows a model of mediation blindly, without understanding and using the theories on which it is based, is like a computer user who cannot type a letter if the word processing application does not function. Mediators who understand their own theory bases are like the skilled computer specialist, who can work directly with the code for the operating system. Core values and beliefs are central to mediators' work; they undergird and support the theories adopted and the models and approaches the mediator uses. As much as possible, mediators should try to obtain internal consistency between their deep personal and professional beliefs, theories, and values and the specific models and methods they use. The more mediators can articulate their deepest beliefs and theories, the more they can evaluate their levels of integration and internal consistency.

Levels of Organization

To understand their constellations of theories, mediators must first understand the characteristics of and differences among facts and information, models, abstract and unifying theories, and core theories, beliefs, and values. In addition to defining these terms, it is useful to explore the levels of organization and the functions of these elements (see Figure 5.2).

The outermost ring of organization is the realm of facts and information. Facts and information are the most loosely connected ideas, often collected randomly, and may not necessarily integrate into any particular model. For example, mediators operating in a community mediation program may need information about the topics that are typically the subject of conflicts mediated in the program, such as housing ordinances, dog leash laws, and the requirements of neighborhood covenants. Mediators bargain in the shadow of the law, so they should know the basic laws pertaining to the dispute being mediated. The laws represent standards that may guide the parties' decision making. Also included at this level are such items as agency policies, requirements for screening for domestic violence, and ethical standards.

This information base is usually specific to the type of dispute handled or the context in which the mediator operates. A mediator

Figure 5.2. Levels of Organization of the Constellation of Theories.

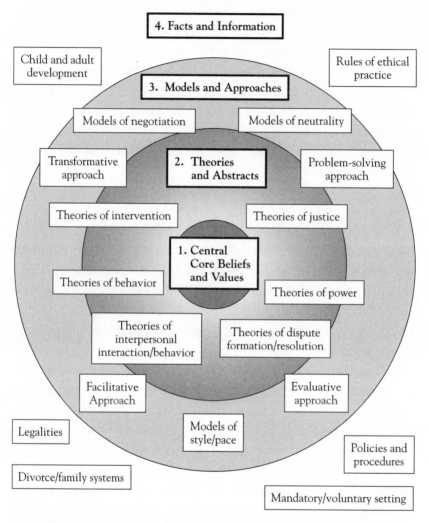

4th ring: Facts and information—sometimes organized, sometimes isolated

3rd ring: Models and approaches—specific ways of doing mediation practice

2nd ring: Theories and abstracts—concepts and unifying theories providing meaning

Center ring: Core values and beliefs—life experiences, spiritual teachings, and personal choices

working with divorce mediation cases may need quality information about child support guidelines, about the relationship of budgets to spousal support, about child development, and about current research results on high-conflict divorce in order to help parties mediate issues related to these topics. Mediators dealing with housing disputes will likely need information about health and safety codes, local ordinances, and the legal requirements of leases. To mediate workplace disputes, mediators should understand employment practices, personnel policies, equal employment opportunity regulations, and other important facts.

The outer ring in Figure 5.2 also includes information about the particular context or setting in which the mediation takes place. For example, mediators practicing in a community mediation center may need information that is unique to that setting and center, such as how to complete the required forms, how to use the phone system, how to work the word processing system, and when and how to make referrals. Mediators generally hold large quantities of information in the outer ring of their constellation. But to function effectively, they must also develop the other rings in the constellation. A practitioner who has learned or can speak to only this level of their constellation is not able to access and utilize the constellation fully. Unfortunately, administrative supervision and training programs often focus only on this ring. Facts alone are not all a mediator needs to understand. Facts remain fragmented and isolated unless they are integrated into models of practice and related to the concepts and practices that are part of the other rings in the constellation.

The next level of organization is more internally consistent and more comprehensive than mere facts. Located at this level are models and approaches—the actual ways of doing mediation and negotiation that the mediator understands and uses. Models show us ideal or best practices, or specific practices for specific populations or problems. The therapeutic mediation model developed by Irving and Benjamin (1995), for example, is a model because it says what is important in practice, why it should be done, and most important, how to do it. Models are fairly broad prescriptions, imperatives, and guidelines for practice that follow a certain base logic and may be applied narrowly to specific populations, problems, or contexts.

Mediators may learn a number of models, but sometimes they select a particular model because it is well suited to a specific context or type of dispute, or because it is consistent with the mediator's beliefs, values, and principles (the other rings in the constellation). In fact, mediators often select a model because it embraces certain abstract qualities and unifying theories. For example, a mediator may have been influenced by the interest-based negotiation model (Fisher and Ury, 1983), or he may follow another, very different model of distributive negotiation, derived from experience in bargaining in the streets of Tijuana, at the backyard garage sale, or in prior business negotiations. The model selected by the mediator for a particular case will depend on the formulation of the case (described in Chapter Four), as well as on the mediator's theories and values. Both models are available to the mediator, but the mediator will select one on the basis of a desire for consistency between the principles of the model and the theories in the mediator's constellation.

Family mediators may rely on a model that proposes that they use one or more of the following four modes of practice: rational-analytic, educative, therapeutic, and normative-evaluative. They may decide to use certain of the modes on the basis of their formulation of the case. The model gives them some idea of when and how to switch from one mode to another. It is a model because it tells the mediator when, how, and why to use the suggested behaviors. This model of mediation practice is context specific, because mediators in other contexts, such as labor mediation, may not see the relevance or value of some of these modes, especially the therapeutic. This model of mediation, then, is useful only for some contexts and in some cases. Mediators practicing in other contexts would need other models in their constellations of theories in order to be flexible and adaptable.

Models represent appropriate, aspirational, or best practices; they include guidelines for implementing them. Most novice mediators learn a particular model and approach to mediation that encompasses guidelines, rules, procedures, and ways of understanding mediation practice. As stated in the chapters on artistry, however, mediators may add to, alter, or otherwise adjust their models when their experiences in practice are not fully explained by the models. Mediators who find their models inadequate or incomplete need to read more about other models and approaches, and to discuss the issue with other mediators to develop a more suitable and relevant model of practice.

To use an analogy: all physicians practice medicine, yet in treating disease some of them employ aggressive approaches such as surgery, radiation, and chemotherapy; others rely on extensive testing before proposing an intervention, and still others rely less on drugs and prescribe lifestyle changes, natural remedies, emotional healing, or support groups. They may all have similar training but their practices differ widely. Their models of practice are based on their theories about medicine and health, about disease, treatment, and prevention. The practice of mediation is similarly enriched by having multiple models, all of which meet basic criteria for competent and ethical practice. Mediation practice will become more diverse and exciting as new models are developed. This diversity leaves much room for personal and professional growth and development. To practice competently and to proceed along the path toward artistry, mediators must adopt and consistently apply at least one comprehensive model of practice but be open to new models to match specific practice needs.

Underlying these models, in a ring nearer the core, are even broader and deeper ideas that support the creation and use of models—theories. A theory explains phenomena—things that are happening or being experienced. The goal of a theory is to give meaning and structure to events, patterns, observations, and behaviors, to be predictive, and sometimes to describe what to expect. Theories are usually highly organized and internally consistent.

The simpler yet more explanatory a theory is, the better it will be in explaining and making meaning for diverse situations. Theories that say a lot but do so succinctly are considered elegant; they represent clarity with simplicity. For example, the theory of relativity explains a lot in a few letters ($E = mc^2$).

Some theories attempt to become universal or unifying in their simplicity and explanation. Rummel (1991) has written an excellent book that articulates a set of principles that taken together make a unifying theory of interpersonal, social, and international conflict and cooperation. It is one of the most elegant and comprehensive unifying theories we have found so far. Beginning with conflict and the individual, then moving to how conflict develops between and among individuals, Rummel's theory explains how individuals participate in the life cycle of a conflict, and how conflicts can be dealt with by differently constructed societies. Galtung (1996) has also articulated basic, unifying constructs and theories for peace and conflict, and Kriesberg (1998) has outlined his theory of how conflicts emerge and resolve. These unifying and basic theories help us make sense of what we are doing and give us the big picture into which we can fit individual disputes. Mediators really need these theoretical underpinnings, on which they build specific models and to which they connect facts and information. Many practitioners have never been formally introduced to the type of theory they need. Mediators who seek to enrich the quality of their practices and who aspire to artistry should enlarge their constellations of theories by finding and integrating new theories into them. We have included some good resources for this exploration in the Resources section at the end of the book.

Mediators' constellations include theories not only about the nature of conflict and dispute resolution but also about human behavior, negotiation, power, neutrality, and the abstract aspects of mediation. They deal with these phenomena in most mediation. Although they may not be able to point to a specific author or source, most mediators do have some type of belief system or theory base from which they operate that may be either fragmented, incomplete, or fully explanatory. For many mediators, the theories in their constellations are often bits and pieces discovered in one source or another; they may be ideas needing more thought and organization. Mediators have found these pieces in training sessions, courses, and books. They have gathered and synthesized them one by one from their experiences. Ask mediators about their theories of negotiation or problem solving and they may struggle to answer, yet in their practices they routinely help unsophisticated disputants learn to bargain and problem solve more effectively. Although many mediators have difficulty articulating their theories, these conceptual structures operate continually, often invisibly, but with certainty. A task of reflective practitioners is to know consciously the theories that guide and shape their behavior.

Unifying and basic theories rest on something even more fundamental: the core beliefs and values that each mediator brings to the profession. These beliefs and values are deeply rooted theories that all people carry with them that help them to explain complex, abstract ideas such as truth, justice, love, fairness, and trust. These core theories are developed early in life and are grounded in experience. Few people other than philosophy majors and those pursuing spiritual and religious disciplines tend to concentrate formally on these great truths and abstracts.

At the center of the constellation of theories is a person's view of life, their foundational values, their orientation to humankind. Although some people become mediators because of their deeply held religious or social values and their views of humanity, other mediators are unaware of their central beliefs and how they inform their perception of events, people, and life. Thomas Sowell (1987) has written an excellent book outlining his premise that inherent in our American democracy is a schism between two dominant world views, which he calls the *constricted* and *unconstricted* views of mankind. Both of these opposing views are valid, but they fuel the constant societal conflicts, because both are promoted in our society simultaneously. This schism of views may also apply to mediators. Those who believe that people have inherent tendencies toward evil, chaos, or negative behavior (the constricted view) might well try to exert control in the mediation process by creating rules and contingencies or by adopting a mediation model that relies on directive and controlling interventions. Mediators who hold the unconstricted view and believe that disputants can be trusted to find their own solutions do not try either indirectly or directly to influence the disputants' decisions or to impose a solution on them. Deep core values, beliefs, and views necessarily influence to some degree all of a person's other theories, models, and facts, because all people tend to collect in their constellation things that are part of a set, that are consistent with the other items in their collection of ideas.

Another analogy that explains the concept of core values and their influence on the other rings in the constellation of theories is derived from the solar system. Each person has a central sun, or core theory, around which the planets of other theories, beliefs, concepts, and facts swirl. This solar system of theories is unique to each person, although many planets or moons may be shared with other mediators. A mediator may believe in the intrinsic worth of all people, and from that core belief may grow the idea of restorative rather than retributive justice. From there, the mediator may be attracted to or find value in ideas of integrative rather than distributive negotiation, and from that set of theories might flow the model of facilitative rather than evaluative process. The mediator may then adopt models of mediation that are transformative rather than problem solving in approach. Even information at the farthest edges of the constellation should be consistent with the core beliefs and other theories. For example, a mediator who believes in the intrinsic worth of the individual ought to try to implement policies and procedures in their context that support voluntary rather than mandatory mediation. That way, he or she can practice in a way that allows enough time to adequately explore the topics and gives the individual the freedom of choice that is supported by the deep value rather than just push for a quick agreement. If all the planets line up in this way, if there is genuine consistency, a truly wonderful, harmonious belief system will contribute to an internal consistency that can be seen externally in the mediator's behavior during interactions, leading to more artistry in practice. In this way, theory informs, guides, and informs practice.

Although no two mediators have exactly the same ideas and the same exposure to models and theories, as the field of mediation grows more regularized and professionalized, trainers, academic programs, and mediators themselves will have more standardized "planets" (bodies of knowledge and theory). Understanding what is basic to mediation theory and practice will still allow for personalization of theories, models, and values. The field will continue to embrace diversity of thought, but will be supported by a core of central facts, knowledge, and theory.

A prospective mediation intern stated in her interview that she was interested in becoming a family mediator because it "resonated" with her inner beliefs about how people should relate to and deal with conflict. As she put it, "I want my work to reflect who I am and what I believe. I want my practice to be consistent with who I am as a person." In aspiring to artistry, mediators become aware of their constellation of theories, reflect on the relationship among the elements within that constellation, and seek consistency and congruence between the theories that inform their practice and the actual implementation of those practices. When the rings of their constellations are aligned, beginning with core beliefs and values, mediators can attain artistry in their practices.

How Integrated Are Your Rings?

Some theories held by mediators may be inconsistent with other elements in their constellation of theories—with their values, worldview, models, or other theories. For example, it is hard to believe that all people are sinful and still mediate impartially, working equally hard for each disputant. It is hard to value the wisdom of elders and yet practice without regard to precedent or history. To believe in adherence to legal principles of due process and procedural justice but then use a model that encourages individuals to make their own decisions without regard to legislation or case law creates tension and discord.

As mediators reflect on and examine the inner logic of the ideas and models they embrace and become aware of inconsistencies between and among them, they identify gaps in their constellations. Mediators often have (but may not be aware of) conflicting or disparate beliefs; they may believe that disputants know best how to resolve their conflict, yet they may use an evaluative mediation approach that implies that the mediator rather than the disputants is the expert. Mediators may not have complete consistency among all of the rings of their constellation, and when they experience internal conflicts they should examine those conflicts and determine which theory or belief will govern in the given situation. Such choice is a sign of ethical, reflective mediation practice and leads to artistry.

For example, a mediator who has a basic belief that clients in mediation know and are entitled to act in their own best interests yet holds to a model of mediation practice in which the mediator closely directs the clients and structures all the interactions will likely experience an internal conflict. But sometimes mediators are so oblivious to the elements in their constellation that they fail to recognize when the uncertainty they are experiencing is the result of an internal conflict. Returning to the analogy of the solar system, mediators who operate from a mind-set that is pre-Copernican do not know what is at the core of their constellation and how the elements in their constellation relate to their core values and beliefs. They cannot see the planets, moons, and asteroids swirling around that central sun. Getting more in touch with their constellation of theories and understanding the theories that emanate from their central, deep beliefs is critical to self-analysis and reflection. Reflection then leads to awareness and to the ability to make conscious, deliberate choices in mediation practice.

Discovering New Planets

In reflecting on their constellations, mediators may distinguish those elements that have been formed in the crucible of their mediation experiences and those that are the product of courses, training, readings, or other learning experiences. Through this reflective process, they may discover that they have a new planet in their constellation, a body of knowledge or theoretical approach that has emerged or that is in the formative stage. Growing out of the mediator's experience and grounded in the interactions of mediation sessions, this new idea represents the natural evolutionary process that suggests that the mediator is moving beyond the rule set of a mediation model he or she learned as a novice. This new perspective, principle, or approach is part of the progressive process of professional development that is part of the growth of artistry. These emerging ideas may develop out of the mediator's experience of a surprising and troubling situation for which the customary approaches were not relevant, or they may result from the mediator's participation in educational programs or from reading the growing body of literature. Most importantly, this growth signifies the mediator's commitment to curiosity, ongoing exploration, and discovery. Those who would aspire to artistry face a challenge in keeping up with the rapidly expanding body of literature and with the flourishing and rich array of practice applications, but it is imperative that a reflective mediator do so in order to develop and evolve their constellation of theories.

Mediators seeking new theories and models will find a rich source of ideas in their own experience. Reflecting on their mediation activities, mediators can learn how their current theories are useful, inadequate, or not helpful. For example, during reflective supervision following a simulated mediation, a student mediator, Sally, was asked to identify her operating system or theory and the specific model of mediation she was using in order to understand the strategy she had implemented in the mediation. Sally found that she could not explain the basis for her intervention in the role-play. As we have learned from working with very practiced and skilled mediators, a mediator's initial reaction that no guiding theory or constellation is at work is not at all unusual.

We took Sally through a reflective process that allowed her to see that she had been very carefully following a script that she had been taught in her initial mediation training. She had learned that expressions of emotion impair their ability to work constructively in solving their problems, and that whenever she saw disputants engage in an escalating emotional exchange, she should intervene in order to lower the emotional temperature. This highly structured model of mediation relied on an internal logic that said, "If I only follow the format and do not deviate, then the clients will come to an agreement." The problem she had experienced during the simulated mediation arose when she intervened (as she had been taught) to reduce the tension of the disputants' conversation. Rather than feeling relief that the mediator was actively engaging in their conversation, the disputants felt that the mediator had interrupted their discussion. It was this comment from the disputants that led to Sally's questioning her model.

Finding the inner logic of the model of mediation she had been following was a liberating experience for Sally, because it gave her room to question and doubt what she had taken as a universal truth. She felt relieved that she was able to question the internal logic of the model she had followed because her experience had shown her that following the script did not always lead to agreements and she had no other way of making sense of how disputants responded to her interventions. Her inability to explain what she had been experiencing had felt very uncomfortable because it had put her into internal conflict. She was saying to herself, "I need to follow the format, but it doesn't seem to be working; but I am supposed to make it work, so therefore there must be something wrong with me as a mediator." She very much wanted to do what the model told her to do, but she felt at a total loss when the proscribed strategy did not produce the intended results. She had felt frustrated, sad, and disempowered and had blamed herself for bad practice when the problem was not her skills but a model that was too limiting and did not take into account the uniqueness of each situation and of the disputants.

When this belief was called into question through the reflective process, Sally was able to say her truth, which was that the highly structured format of her mediation model only sometimes led clients into agreement. Sally also realized that she needed more theory, understanding, and information in order to develop additional models that would explain the behavior of disputants and provide additional strategies for assisting clients in moving toward agreement. She learned that she needed more planets in her constellation.

Reflective practice provides the methods for questioning operating beliefs and practices and for assessing the relevance, utility, and value of these approaches. Mediators using the principles and methods of reflective practice learn to develop new approaches and to weed out those theories that no longer fit.

Where Is the Edge of the Known World for You?

Working with the constellation of theories in training seminars, we have found that some mediators are clear about their central, core values and beliefs but are less certain about the theories in the next ring that affect their professional practices. Some practitioners have very clear and well-articulated models but find it difficult to map out their core beliefs about abstract concepts such as restorative justice, fairness, and neutrality. They simply have not thought about these matters. Other mediators are solidly grounded in their fact base and have no unifying theory or discernable, articulated model or approach to mediation; they just do what feels right. These mediators lack a coherent, articulated, and congruent set of theories to guide their practices. To achieve artistry in practice, mediators must operate from a well-established, explicit, integrated, and functional theory base.

It has been said that given the history of its development, mediation is a practice in search of a theory. Because practitioners tend to gather bits of knowledge in somewhat random ways, many practitioners have a hodgepodge collection of theories that are either disparate or loosely strung together. Until recently, no comprehensive academic programs or other efforts identified the core theories and practice skills of mediation; as a result there has been no consensus about the essential readings, concepts, theories, and principles of mediation, with the exception of ethical standards. Like intellectual islands, the mediator's theories and fragments of models continue to develop as separate entities that do not connect, integrate, or support one another. Many mediators do not have mental bins in which to discern, sort, and explain their experiences and collections of information.

As mediators increasingly search for cohesive and comprehensive theories in which to ground their practices and as they attempt to articulate the essential principles of mediation practice, new explanations will emerge. Two important beginning steps in this direction are for mediators to articulate their constellations of theory and to utilize the methods of reflective practice.

In the past ten years, concepts, theories, and models that explain conflict emergence and resolution, collaborative processes, restorative justice, third-party intervention, and negotiation itself have become clearer and more articulated. A mediator in search of a more expansive constellation of theories can find a number of well-outlined models and theoretical perspectives. When mediators find the unifying principles and models that bring together and give coherence to the collection of concepts and processes they have gathered over time, they have a more comprehensive and coordinated way of viewing their practices. Our goal in this book is not necessarily to change what a mediator believes but rather to encourage mediators to make their theory base, their operating system, broader, more interdisciplinary, and more capable of responding to complex issues. Through reflection and by bringing into harmony the essential connections between theory and practice, between beliefs and action, mediators can enlarge and enrich their constellations, leading to a more clearly articulated understanding of the foundations of their practice.

Inspiration Versus Intuition and Insight

When asked why they chose a particular intervention or strategy in working with clients, many mediators state that they "just had a hunch" or that they "had an intuition" about the situation. In reflective supervision sessions, mediators are usually able to see that what they had been calling intuition—that sense of sudden clarity and understanding either from inside themselves or from outside sources—was really the result of their ability to operate from complex and deep layers of theory and knowledge. Seemingly intuitive responses by mediators are also grounded in perceptiveness, empathy with clients, and the ability to understand and appreciate the potential of the situation. In addition, intuitive responses are the result of well-grounded formulations as well as mediators' ability to access and use their constellations of theories at appropriate times. Mediators acting intuitively are able to be fully available to their clients during interactions—something we discuss at length in Part Three of this book.

Mediators who experience sudden bursts of intuition are in reality able to bring their theoretical base to bear on the information offered by the disputants, and thus to respond more fully or artfully. Sometimes this intuitive experience results from a sudden awareness of how the reality of the disputants' conflict situation relates to an element in the mediator's constellation of theories. Sometimes it results from a spontaneous change in the mediator's formulation that then leads to highly effective interventions. The sensation of suddenly making sense of disputants' experience feels like an intuition, but it really flows from the integration of theory and practice. Intuition is the synthesis of theory with knowledge gained in the interaction that guides the mediator's behavior, resulting in skillful, artistic responses. Through reflective process, the mediator can usually go back to those moments of so-called intuition to uncover the theory on which the hunch was made. Focusing through reflective practice on his or her thoughts leading up to the intuitive moment helps the mediator to identify what clicked into place.

To uncover the source of intuition requires not only willingness to engage in the methods of reflective practice but also yearning to advance one's understanding of the burst of insight that results from the strong and clear connection between theory and practice. Through practice and with intention, mediators can deconstruct the mediation process, as illustrated in Chapter One, identifying the elements of skill and knowledge as well as the theories and principles that were essential to the mediator's arriving at the intuition to intervene in helpful ways. Intuition appears magical, out of the mediator's control, and truly disarming. In fact, what passes for intuition is a form of artistry, and as noted previously, artistry can be defined, understood, and learned, especially as mediators reflect on their constellations of theories that are guiding them.

How to Map Your Constellation

Most mediators find that it is easier to understand their constellation of theories by starting with the "sun"—their core beliefs about people, their values, and their overarching worldview. From the center they can then elaborate on the rings of their solar system. Others may find it more helpful to start with the outer edges of their constellation, where facts and information reside, and work inward to find their models, then their theories, and finally their core beliefs. We have observed, during mapping exercises in workshops, that most mediators find some levels easier or more challenging to articulate than others. This is normal, because that which is familiar is easier to acknowledge, and what is undiscovered or less well known seems elusive.

Because constellations of theories, by their very nature, are complex and interconnected, mapping them can be a challenging enterprise. It is important to take the time to chart your mental solar system. By identifying and claiming what you know, you can fully access your constellations at important moments in order to create, change, or expand formulations, or to give clarity and meaning to disputants' interactions. Though this task may seem like a scholastic effort not required of practicing mediators, full comprehension of your constellation of theories is vital to competent, resourceful, and artistic practice.

Walking the Path of Artistry

Here are some questions you can ask yourself to get more in touch with your unique constellation. Though some of these questions are framed in an either-or form, there may be many more answers than two.

Begin with a large sheet of paper, as big as a desk or a door, and draw four concentric circles (as in Figure 5.2). Label them as follows:

- Outside ring: Facts and information
- Next ring in: Models and approaches
- Third ring in: Theories—unifying, abstract concepts
- Center ring: Core values and views

Then, write your answers to the following questions on separate sticky notes. If you do not have an answer, write the question and put a question mark on the sticky note. Then put each sticky note on the constellation rings where you think it belongs. You may move them around, combine them by sticking them together, or change your answers.

Core Beliefs

- Are people here to meet their own needs, or to serve others?
- Are people inherently weak and bad, needing correction, or are they inherently good and able to respond positively?

- Is the individual subservient to the group, society, or organization, or is the group, society, or organization here to meet the needs of the individual?
- What is the relationship of individuals to the larger system in which they exist?
- What did I learn in my family about methods for handling conflict?
- In what do I put my trust and faith?
- What are my beliefs about justice and fairness?
- What are my moral values and what are their sources?

Theories That Unify and Explain Abstract Concepts

- What is my view about how conflict emerges and is dealt with?
- What is legitimate coercive power in society? Can that ever change?
- What do I think demonstrates fairness?
- What forms the basis of personal and group authority? Is that the same as power?
- Can individuals make up their own rules and fairness concepts, or should society or government make up the rules?
- Is coercion ever justifiable? Is violence? Is war ever just?
- What are the sources of personal, organizational, national, and international power?

Models of Mediation and Negotiation

- What models and conceptual frameworks did I bring from my background or prior profession or professions?
- What was the name of the model of mediation, negotiation, or facilitation I first learned? How would I describe the methods and strategies presented in this model?

- What is the basic internal logic of this model of mediation, expressed as, "If . . . and if . . ., then. . . "?
- What are the limitations of this model?
- What does my model say about the role of intervenor?
- What is the stated goal of this model?
- What phenomena does my model not explain?
- When I am working as a (mediator) I must. . . .
- When I am working as a (mediator) I cannot. . . .
- What experiences have I had that confirm this model?
- What experiences have I had that do not fit with this model?

Facts and Information

- What state and national laws pertain to my type of mediation?
- What standards of practice do I follow?
- What ethics rules must I follow?
- What are the controversial issues in my field?

When you have placed all of the sticky notes in the rings, look for patterns, gaps, and redundancies. Then list three words that come to mind when you look at the center ring. These words should be adjectives or nouns.

When you look at the third ring, theory, list the three qualities you care about most.

When you look at the second ring, models of practice, list three verbs that you derive from what you see.

When you look at the outer ring, count the number of sticky notes.

Then, looking at your responses to these instructions, state to yourself the following:

- What I care most about as a mediator is _____ .
- The way I want to practice is _____ .
- My professional disclosure to clients should include _____ .
- My constellation is adequate/not adequate.

Walking the Path: Learning from Success and Failure Stories

I. Success Stories
    A. Write a success story of a mediation case. Be sure to state why you think it was successful. In addition, be sure to note the outcome of the mediation.
    B. Now write about the following three areas:
        1. Your formulation of the case—about the people, the problem, and the process needed
        2. What actually happened—as either a chronology or a narrative ("and then . . ., and then . . .)
        3. How you felt about yourself as a mediator during and then after the case
    C. Next, review the information and answer the following questions:
        1. If I were to tell a novice mediator what was important about what I did, what would I emphasize?
        2. What patterns emerged?
    D. Look the information over again and state to yourself:
        For a person to have done this, they would have to
            Believe _____ about people in general
            Understand the abstract concepts of _____
            Have a worldview or conceptual framework that most resembles _____
            Think _____ about conflict resolution and mediation processes
            Use a model of mediation that could be called _____
            Have sufficient information about _____

This exercise should give you some idea of the constellation you were using when you were working well.

II. Failure Stories
    A. Write a horror story about the failure of a mediation case that you have had. Be sure to state why you think it was a failure or horrible experience. Make sure you include the outcome of the mediation.
    B. Go through the same set of questions you used for the success story.

This exercise should give you some idea of the constellation of theories you used when you were working poorly.

Finally, figure out what, if anything, was different between your success and your failure stories.

Looking Back, Looking Forward

By the time mediators move from novice to apprentice to practitioner, their collection of models and concepts, as part of their constellations of theory, should be well established, thick, and rich, and accessible to them upon reflection. Mediators need to know what they know, and through what lenses of information, theory, and belief they view specific case formulations and interactions. The constellation of theories is unique to each mediator. It will be part of what is functioning in the room during the interaction, and part of what the mediator needs to reflect on both during (in action) and after (on action) the session.

Mediators cannot help but see the world in ways that are familiar and comfortable. The constellation of theories gives mediators many lenses through which to look at people and disputes. They bring their constellation of theories, or as Rummel (1991) calls it, their "socio-cultural space," with them, and they are guided by and operate out of that set of core beliefs, theories, models, and information.

Mediators should share their formulations, and at times their foundations, with disputants, allowing them to obtain a fresh perspective on their conflict and themselves. This sharing can bring about transformation of the parties, reshape the interaction and power bases of interaction, and reframe issues, concerns, and attributions that have been operating between the parties.

The goals of reflective practitioners are to learn about and have access to the beliefs, values, and overarching ways of seeing the world that shape their practices. The more they can utilize this knowledge, bringing it into the mediation role, they better chance they will have of achieving a more flexible, responsive, resourceful, and artistic practice. In the next chapter we more fully explore the nature and process of reflection as the way to uncover and utilize formulations and constellations of theories to create artistry.

Chapter Six

Putting Reflection into Practice

The principles and methods of reflective practice that we have developed have deep historical roots. The notion that people will think about their circumstances and reflect on the problems they confront is not novel.

The tradition of reflection is venerable and extends deep into both western and eastern traditions. Cultures that value creativity, ingenuity, and innovation honor divergent thinkers for their ability to question convention and offer unique approaches to social concerns. Today's culture also values the individual who is neither wedded to convention nor limited in his or her vision by the past—whose understanding of the past and whose openness to different ways of looking at problems results in ingenious solutions that at once seem both obvious and profound. Whether in science, the arts, politics, or sports, our society honors the person who contributes a novel and innovative approach to common situations and problems.

In a quest to understand the distinctive qualities and characteristics that define the creative, innovative mind, we questioned whether there is a distinctive path that the person with such a mind follows and whether that person possesses unique talents, intelligence, physical gifts, or insights. Our journey led us to the conclusion that the capacity for reflection, as a component of artistry, can be developed through a course of study and enhanced through a disciplined approach to practice. Guided initially by notions about reflective practice that were originally proposed by Donald Schön (1983, 1987) and by Schön and Chris Argyris (1974), we have created a set of principles and methods that can build the reflective skills necessary for the practitioner's journey along the path toward artistry.

In this chapter we present methods and techniques of reflective practice for increasing the effectiveness of mediation. We describe the practices we use to train professional mediators in the techniques and principles of reflective practice and we introduce a process for building competency and professionalism that enriches the quality of professional experiences and leads to artistry in practice.

We use the term *reflective practice* to denote the ability to think divergently, to be unfettered by the limits of conventional wisdom, and to accept the challenge of the novel circumstance to develop a new approach or analysis. Schön has described reflective practice as a process through which "both ordinary people and professionals think about what they are doing, sometimes even while doing it. . . . They may ask themselves, for example, 'What features do I notice when I recognize this thing? What are the criteria by which I make this judgment? What procedures am I enacting when I perform this skill? How am I framing the problem that I am trying to solve?'" (1983, p. 50).

We believe that individuals can learn the discipline of reflection and through that process access their creative potential and achieve artistry in practice. We focus here on the process by which individuals move from the ordinary to the unique, from the mundane to the sublime, from the conventional to the innovative.

The Nature of Reflective Practice

At the heart of reflective practice is the willingness to question, to explore, to delve into the unknown and the uncertain. This chapter is organized around questions that explore and investigate the principles and methods of reflective practice. We asked ourselves these questions as we studied the concept of artistry in professional practice, and we encourage our students and colleagues to ask them as they think about their own practices. We use questions to explore the terrain of what we know and to identify and investigate what is presently unknown, to evaluate and make sense of our professional experiences and the impact of our work on our clients, to understand the principles by which we function as practitioners, and to seek out new information about the ways we approach the challenges and tasks of professional practice. As we have noted, questions are at the heart of both the reflective approach we take as practitioners and the method we use as teachers of mediators. They are the building blocks of an interactive process. Throughout the book we have posed questions that encourage reflection, inviting you to think about the implications for your practices and for the training and education of professional mediators of the ideas and methods we have presented.

We begin here with a definition of reflective practice, including a discussion of the origins of our interpretation of the concepts and practices involved in this discipline. We explain our beliefs about the principles and methods of reflective practice, and we link our notions to the writings of others whose work has contributed to our understanding of these concepts and approaches. Finally, we present a number of tools and techniques for developing the mindset of a reflective practitioner, and we describe their use in professional practice.

Defining Reflective Practice

Schön (1983, 1987) examined the concept of what it means to be a competent professional by asking "what is the kind of knowing in which competent practitioners engage"(1983, p. viii). Mediators continually make decisions about how to structure the process they are guiding, choosing when to ask for a private session, how to respond to the differing ways that clients interact, when and how to assist clients in their conversations about difficult topics, whether to use questions, and what types to use. Our quest to understand artistry and the path that leads to professional competence was stimulated by an interest in understanding how mediators know when to use the strategies and techniques that make up their repertoire of professional skills. We were curious about the cues and clues that guide a mediator's choice of strategies and techniques. It seemed to us that because artistry is reflected in the type, timing, and nature of interventions, it is important to understand the process by which a mediator makes these choices.

Mediators, to a very great extent, have learned a series of responses to particular situations, a repertoire of techniques and strategies that, if effectively implemented, allow them to assist disputing parties in recognizing, understanding, and dealing with their conflicts. For many whose practices involve primarily one type of conflict situation, the repertoire of skills serves them well in responding to the predictable events that occur in mediating such conflicts. Mediators learn, for example, that convening private sessions is one of the tools for responding to clients who are caught in an escalating spiral of recrimination, accusation, and blame. The belief that supports this intervention is that a caucus will allow each party to give full expression to the frustrations inherent in the conflict, in a setting free from the reactions and responses of the other party.

The ability to recognize when a private session may be helpful is an indicator of basic mediator competency. Mediators learn through training and experience that private sessions are helpful to parties in certain situations. Some mediators respond to the expression of strong emotions out of habit, almost automatically convening private sessions. Others weigh and evaluate the circumstances, looking for what may be unique in the parties' interactions, remaining open to the possibility that the parties might not benefit from private sessions, and making decisions about convening a caucus by taking into account a wide array of data. The first group are competent, responsible mediators, whom we have called practitioners in our dynamic four-stage model of professional development (see Chapter One). The second group, by contrast, are demonstrating the principles of reflective practice. They are deliberate, analytical, and curious, able to discern unconventional solutions to problems. They employ the methods of reflective practice to achieve artistry.

To understand the mental process by which the mediator makes these decisions, it is necessary to identify the information that mediators use to guide their practice decisions, to understand what they observed in the parties' interactions that warranted attention and response, and to learn how their understanding of the conflict and its context led to the decision to implement a particular strategy or technique. Exploring this terrain is at the heart of the process of reflective practice that mediators implement in developing artistry in their practices.

Characteristics of Reflective Practitioners

What are the qualities and characteristics of a reflective practitioner? What attitudes, beliefs, and practices distinguish a reflective practitioner from other practitioners? In our experience, the following characteristics differentiate the basically competent mediator from the artistic mediator who applies the principles and methods of reflective practice:

- They engage in a continual process of self-reflection (reflecting in action and reflection on action).
- They rely on theory to guide and inform their practice.
- They use the process of experimentation to test their observations, perceptions, and formulations of the experiences, beliefs, and needs of their clients.
- They are willing to see perspectives other than their own, to experience surprise.
- They are open to new information about their practices; lifelong learners, they are open to new strategies and techniques.
- They do not see themselves as experts, but they acknowledge that both they and their clients have expertise to bring to bear on the conflict situation.

The following story illustrates a number of the principles and characteristics of reflective practice. The coaching exchange described here occurred during a role-play debriefing, with the coach asking the mediator questions that explored the nature, purpose, and effect of the mediator's interventions. Early in the mediation, as the parties were invited to tell their stories, the mediator attentively listened to and then effectively summarized the first party's (Ralph's) story. The second party (Beatrice) was then invited to describe the concerns that underlie the conflict, and she did so. Before the mediator could summarize Beatrice's story, the disputants began talking directly with each other in a constructive though emotional manner about their positions and concerns.

After observing their conversation for several minutes, the mediator interrupted the disputants and summarized what Beatrice had said. At this moment the coach stopped the role-play and engaged in the following dialogue with the mediator:

> *Coach:* What was happening in the mediation that influenced your decision to intervene here, and what did you hope to achieve?
>
> *Mediator:* I realized that I had not summarized what Beatrice had said. I was taught that summarizing helps to clarify the story, to make a connection with each party, and to build trust. I wanted to be sure the mediation didn't go too far without my being able to establish rapport with both disputants.
>
> *Coach:* Would you be interested in asking Beatrice about her experience of you as the mediator, and whether trust was an issue for her?
>
> *Mediator:* Yes. I wondered what she was thinking when I didn't summarize her story as I had for Ralph.
>
> *Beatrice:* I felt no lack of connection from the mediator. I could see that she was being attentive when I spoke. She seemed interested in what I had to say. She seemed to be a good listener.
>
> *Coach (to mediator):* What do you make of this information?

Mediator: It makes me feel much better in a way. I was unsure whether I was connecting with her. I really didn't have a sense that there was a problem with Beatrice, but I had been taught to summarize, so that's what was causing some concern. In thinking about the situation, I guess I was uncertain how to control the process. I didn't know whether I needed to do anything about the way they were talking with each other; they seemed pretty angry. I was afraid I might not be able to help them if their discussion got more heated. So, to limit the emotion of their conversation, I went back to something I knew how to do, which is summarizing.

Coach: You seem to be aware of something you hadn't been when we started to talk. Does this awareness about your reaction to the heated discussion lead you to any conclusions about yourself as a mediator?

Mediator: Well, I can see that I need to understand more about the mediator's role in managing the mediation. I didn't know whether I should intervene when they were raising their voices. So I would like to understand my role when this happens, and I want to learn other ways to deal with strong emotions.

The dialogue continued. The coach next focused on the mediator's concern that the heated discussion might spin out of control, and he invited the mediator again to involve the disputants. The mediator learned new information from Ralph and Beatrice that challenged her assumptions about the risk of an emotional conversation. Using that information, the mediator applied the reflective process to consider a different set of responses when faced with a similar situation.

This interaction between coach and student reveals a learning approach and teaching method that are markedly different from the methods used in most mediation training programs. The emphasis in this exchange was on the mediator's learning rather than on the demonstration of the coach's expertise. The questions were structured to encourage reflection. The focus of the exchange was on the mediator's exploration of her experience; the coach helped the mediator probe the mediation for a fresh perspective. The mediator came to understand why she acted as she had, what the implications were, and what alternative approaches she could take in the future.

The coach's questions and the student's responses illustrate the characteristics of reflective practitioners listed earlier:

- *Reflective practitioners engage in a continual process of self-reflection.* Mediators who embrace the methods and principles of reflective practice engage in an ongoing process of reflection, testing their perceptions against the experiences, beliefs, and needs of the disputants. Mediators learn whether the meaning they have given to the information provided by the disputants is accurate, whether their interventions have been helpful, and whether their approach is responsive to the disputants' needs, interests, concerns, and goals.

In the example, the coach highlighted the importance of inviting the parties to assist in the process of examining the relevance, impact, and value of interventions. He invited the mediator to engage the parties in helping the mediator learn about her practices and their effects. With encouragement from the coach, the mediator questioned Beatrice to learn whether she perceived the mediator as having been attentive and connected. Beatrice's feedback dispelled the mediator's belief that she had failed to establish an effective working relationship with Beatrice. As a result the mediator questioned her operating assumption about the methods for developing rapport, which had influenced her decision to interrupt the participants in order to summarize Beatrice's story.

The mediator explored the possible theories and behaviors that would explain this new information. She learned that techniques other than summarizing can produce the desired effect. Establishing rapport requires more than the exercise of specific techniques. Although summarizing indeed helps to create a positive relationship between participants and the mediator, the mediator realized that listening attentively, making eye contact, and other similar gestures may be equally important.

Through self-reflection, the mediator explored the uncertain terrain of the mediation experience, made discoveries, and learned about the theories and principles that shape her practice—the assumptions that guided her decision to interrupt. These beliefs about the role of the mediator were operating largely outside her awareness, but nevertheless they directly influenced her practice choices. By making explicit what had been tacit, by uncovering the operating model that was directing her interventions, the mediator was then able to be purposeful and intentional in her strategy and techniques. When such principles operate in the background, outside the mediator's awareness, she has less control over her practice decisions.

The same process of examination and exploration that we observed during the postsession exchanges between the mediator and the coach also occur during the mediation process, as reflection in action. Reflective practitioners monitor their interventions with the parties; they test their assumptions about the parties' attitudes, reactions, and perceptions, with an openness to learning more about the conflict situation, about the disputants, and about themselves as professionals.

- *Reflective practitioners rely on theory to guide and inform their practice.* Acknowledging the connection between theory and practice is essential to reflective practice. Artists in mediation practice engage in an ongoing process of identifying their constellations of theories and developing and testing their formulations. Mediators who apply the methods and principles of reflective process are curious to know whether their formulation fits the parties' understanding of the conflict, and to learn if their constellation of theories is applicable and relevant to the conflict situation.

In the earlier example, the coach's questions helped the mediator uncover the difference between the theory she had been taught to apply and the theory that was evolving out of her experience in the mediation. In her training, the mediator had learned to summarize a disputant's story during the early phase of the mediation in order to build rapport, develop a sense of trust, and ensure that the mediator had in fact understood what the party said. The theory that supports the use of summarizing techniques holds that a mediator must establish rapport in order to build credibility with the parties and to encourage them to engage in the process with candor. The mediator in this case experienced dissonance between following a theory and practice she had been taught and violating another principle of mediation practice she had learned. She had been taught not to interrupt parties when they are engaged in a constructive though emotional discussion. She faced a dilemma: interrupt the parties and risk the loss of spontaneity and focus, or allow the discussion to continue and risk that one of the parties would not have a suitable rapport with the mediator.

By asking elicitive questions, the coach supported and encouraged the mediator to think about her dilemma when dealing with a situation that did not fit the model she had been taught. The situation was unique, and thus surprising. The mediator felt hampered, unable to construct a useful intervention. But in the course of her reflection, she came to a fresh understanding of her dilemma, and learned why interrupting the parties was not always the most helpful or appropriate intervention. To respond appropriately in circumstances that are surprising and uncertain, a mediator must inquire, explore, and investigate, in order to develop an approach that is responsive to the situation. Relying faithfully and without question on a generalized theory limits the mediator's ability to be creative and responsive. Theories have value; they explain, illuminate, and provide guidance. In this situation, however, the mediator learned to modify the theory and to adjust her interventions according to the behavior of the parties.

• *Reflective practitioners use the process of experimentation to test their observations, perceptions, and formulations of the experiences, beliefs, and needs of their clients.* As the example illustrates, a coach can help a mediator utilize the wisdom, knowledge, and experience of the disputants to test out the mediator's observations and perceptions. Whether the mediator in this case had established rapport could best be learned by asking the disputant. As a result of her inquiry, the mediator was presented with a response that was both comforting ("I felt no lack of connection from the mediator") and confusing. If establishing rapport was the goal, then interrupting the discussion was unnecessary, and potentially counterproductive. With the support of the coach, the mediator then applied this new information, thus enriching her practice skills.

• *Reflective practitioners are willing to see perspectives other than their own, to experience surprise.* Artistic mediators who embrace the principles and methods of reflective practice are explorers seeking new ideas, new information, and new perspectives. They are not locked into a one-dimensional view of the parties and their conflict situation.

The debriefing process relies on elicitive questions that encourage the mediator to explore her experience, to make her own discoveries. The mediator is a learner, investigating uncertain territory with an open mind, curiosity, and an eagerness to gain new ideas and perspectives. With guidance from the coach, the mediator in this case uncovered the purposes behind her interventions, recognized the choice points for possible intervention (after Beatrice's story or as the emotional temperature of the conversation was increasing), and identified the dilemmas she perceived. In the reflective process, she explored the rationale for her decisions. As a result she became aware of her strengths and limitations in areas of skill or knowledge. In addition, by reflecting on her approach, she uncovered additional questions for herself about the role of the mediator, identified techniques for dealing with the expression of strong emotion, and determined how she could both hold onto a set of beliefs about the process and at the same time be flexible enough to respond to unique circumstances.

The elicitive approach helps mediators to appreciate the importance of self-reflection in identifying the reasons underlying their use of a particular intervention, in investigating alternatives that may require new thinking, and most importantly in developing new skills and ways of addressing problems by learning from each experience.

- *Reflective practitioners are open to new information about their practices; lifelong learners, they are open to new strategies and techniques.* Artistic mediators are open to learning about their own practices and to using new information to enhance the quality of their professional work. Openness to learning about oneself and to testing one's ideas, beliefs, and practices is characteristic of reflective practice, and a fundamental attribute of artistry.

The mediator in the example acknowledged that she needed to learn additional skills and needed more supervised practice; she also identified some of the knowledge she needed to gain in order to be a more effective and confident mediator. The coach did not tell her what she did well or poorly, did not identify what she needed to learn, and did not instruct the mediator in how to conduct the mediation more competently. The mediator, by considering the careful, elicitive questions asked by the coach, conducted her own exploration, made her own discoveries, and identified her own strengths and limitations.

The mediator was learning how to reflect on her work, how to discern the areas in which her knowledge and skills were suited to the task, and where she lacked experience, understanding, or techniques. She learned about herself as a mediator and how to evaluate and assess her experiences. The discernment required of an artistic mediator using the methods of reflective practice leads to an exploration of the underlying reasons why the mediator has been successful or why her interventions have not accomplished the results she anticipated. The distinction between knowing what worked or what did not, and understanding why, distinguishes reflective practitioners from other professionals. Many professionals have a wealth of experience; the reflective practitioner not only has experiences, but she also learns from them.

- *Reflective practitioners do not see themselves as experts, but they acknowledge that both they and their clients have expertise to bring to bear on the conflict situation.* The mediator can ask disputants to comment on their experience of the mediation process during the mediation. Engaging in this type of inquiry requires an intention on the part of the mediator to seek such information from the disputants, to encourage and invite their comments and questions. To engage disputants in this manner also requires the mediator to be willing to accept, acknowledge, and incorporate the information received. By inviting the disputants to comment on the mediation process and provide their perspectives, the coach models behavior to the parties that is respectful of their expertise. By recommending this approach to the disputants, the coach invites the mediator to take advantage of and utilize the parties' expertise in the mediator's own process of reflection and exploration.

The mediator in this case was learning to reflect on her work as a mediator, to discern the areas in which her knowledge and skills were suited to the task and those in which she lacked experience, understanding, or techniques. She learned how to evaluate, assess, and make sense of her experiences. Although we encourage self-reflection as an essential feature of a constructive learning process, we eschew the type of self-judgment that simply reflects compliance with or disregard of certain standards but does little to help mediators enhance and enrich their practices. That kind of thinking inhibits curiosity and thoughtful reflection, and seldom leads to meaningful discovery or lasting knowledge. The discernment required of an artist involves disciplined exploration of the underlying reasons why an intervention or strategy has been successful, or why an approach has not accomplished the anticipated results. Artistic mediators are distinguished by their interest in and curiosity about the reasons for success and failure, and by their commitment to the methods and principles of reflective practice.

The mediator in this example began to understand the importance of reflecting on her interventions; she began to examine critically and to explore courageously whether her choices and actions were achieving the intended results. She reflected on the extent to which the theory she had learned was universally applicable and on whether her skills were adequate for dealing with the parties and issues. As she realized the limits of the theory as well as the limits of her knowledge and skills, she also became aware of the importance of reflection in action—of thinking about her actions even as she was implementing an intervention approach.

Reflection in Action

The coach's questioning of the mediator modeled the process of reflecting in the moment, what Schön (1983, 1987) refers to as *reflecting in action*. Reflecting in action is sparked by a response in the course of a mediation to an event, interaction, or other experience that is surprising, unexpected, and out of the routine. "Surprise leads to reflection within an action present. . . . We think critically about the thinking that has got us into this fix or this opportunity; and we may, in the process, restructure strategies of action, understandings of phenomena, or ways of framing problems" (Schön, 1987, p. 28).

Reflecting in action is an internal conversation about the processes, tasks, and strategies that have led the mediation to a point that is confounding, out of the ordinary, or unexpected. It is a method for responding to the elements of interaction (see Chapter Seven) and to critical moments (see Chapter Eight).

Professionals can deepen their understanding of their work and increase their interactive effectiveness with clients by thinking about what they are doing while they are doing it. They are simultaneously engaging with the clients, providing guidance and assistance, and thinking about their own actions and the impact of their interventions on the clients. Mediators use the insights gained through such moment-by-moment exploration of the dispute and the parties' interactions to learn something new about the conflict situation, about the clients and their dispute process, and about how they can utilize their skills to assist the disputants in dealing with their conflict.

Methods for Developing the Practice of Reflection

In our experience as mediators and particularly as teachers and coaches, we have developed a number of exercises that encourage the practice of reflection.

Being Intentional

Be intentional about your practice. Though this maxim may seem simplistic and obvious, in our experience most mediators are not purposeful about their practice. Yes, they make decisions, selecting one form of intervention over another, but intentionality is more than a succession of choices about technique and strategy. To be intentional about one's practice requires the ability to reflect in action, to pay attention to the details of the interaction, and to apply theory to practice. The development of an appropriate mind-set is aided by using the inventories described later in the chapter, by maintaining a learning journal, and by seeking the guidance of a coach.

Elizabeth Langer has written two books, *Mindfulness* (1989) and *The Power of Mindful Learning* (1997), that describe the ability to be present, intentional, and purposeful in our actions and thoughts. To illustrate the perils of mindlessness, Langer recounts an incident that occurred at a retail store when she handed a clerk her credit card to pay for her purchases. The clerk returned the card with a pen, indicating that the author had not yet signed the back of the card. Langer did so and handed the card to the clerk, who processed the transaction. The clerk then compared the signatures on the card and the receipt. Well trained to follow this routine in order to prevent fraud, the clerk acted as if the current situation were like all others she had been trained to process. She failed to recognize the differences, the new information, and as a result, acted mindlessly.

A quality of acting intentionally is mindfulness, the use of our attention to gather and test necessary, useful, and relevant information in order to distinguish instances in which the rules we have learned for a particular situation either do or do not apply.

Making the Connection Between Theory and Practice

At the heart of artistry is a commitment to the notion that theory shapes practice. Mediators who have a rationale for their interventions, who deliberately apply skills with an understanding of their likely impact, and who monitor and evaluate their interventions in light of their predictions are most likely to attain artistry. To function in this way requires a grounding in theory—in the beliefs, principles, and values that support practice—as well a commitment to practice, so that there is congruence between what mediators believe and how they practice.

Theories are vehicles for explanation, prediction, or control. An *explanatory theory* explains events by setting forth propositions from which these events may be inferred, a *predictive theory* sets forth propositions from which inferences about future events may be made, and a *theory of control* describes the conditions under which events of a certain kind may be made to occur (Schön, 1983).

A mediator who does not connect his or her practice skills to theory is merely tinkering with a situation, trying out strategies and techniques without knowledge of why those skills might or might not be appropriate at that time and with the particular disputants, and lacking the ability to evaluate and understand the consequences and results of the interactions. Central to effective and competent practice is awareness of the principles that are the foundation for practice. From that awareness comes the possibility of understanding how one's principles influence, organize, and guide one's professional practice. "Practitioners may be chalking potentially instructive cases up to luck because they do not have the frameworks to do otherwise—to think of and understand these cases on their own terms and to intervene consciously in ways that foster such outcomes" (Bush and Folger, 1994, p. 11). Without an awareness of the reasons why interventions succeed or fail, mediators are like sailboats without rudder and keels—at the mercy of the shifting winds and tides, reacting to situations without the necessary equipment to determine a course. Having a collection of skills and proficiency in their application does not ensure that the skills will be used appropriately and to the best effect. Mediators seek to fill their toolboxes, believing that competency in the use of many tools is the way to achieve effective practice. Although proficiency in the use of a wide array of tools is one of the essential elements of professional practice, the mediator who does not also understand the situations in which such tools are most useful will inevitably be a tinkerer—trying out a succession of tools, unaware of the reasons for using them, and unaware of why those tools have either achieved a desired result or failed to assist the parties.

Theories explain why certain practice tools work in certain circumstances. As an exercise in becoming aware of the values, beliefs, principles, and theories that shape their professional practice (their constellation of theories), we encourage mediators to answer the questions posed in Chapter Five.

A student of ours, Irene McLaughlin, a mediator and a judge, prepared a written piece, reflecting on action, based on her experience as a mediator in a role-play simulation (Amy and Bill; see Chapter Two). She organized her thinking by identifying (1) what she had said, (2) the purpose for her comment or question, (3) what she might have said or the question she might have asked, and (4) the purpose of that alternative comment or question. An excerpt from that paper appears in Exhibit 6.1.

In these examples we can observe how she used the process of reflection on action to identify the critical moments during the mediation, to examine her behavior and its intended purpose. Her reflection then led to considering alternative approaches and the purpose they might serve. She reflected not simply on the techniques she employed but equally as important on the beliefs on which they were based. This example of reflection on action clearly illustrates the value of the reflective process in the development of effective, resourceful mediators.

The ultimate goal of identifying the theories that support practice is to ensure that the application of techniques and strategies is congruent with those theories. When there is consistency between

Said	Purpose	Might Have	Purpose of Alternative
Asked Amy, "Are you being heard?"	Reacting to her obvious discomfort with Bill's behavior while she was tentatively saying, "I am feeling. . . . "	Let Amy struggle with articulating her feelings, perhaps asking an open question such as, "What's going on for you right now?" and if she was able to express her discomfort I would work with that information; if not, then I could ask the original question.	Empowering Amy by providing an opportunity for her to clarify and articulate her discomfort; it might have been too soon to pressure her into articulating her feelings.
Responded to Bill's assertion that his job depended on acquiescence to a mediated agreement by saying, "I don't know that your job does depend on it."	Attempting to remove what to me seemed to be another nonsensical hurdle that Bill kept placing in the way of achieving reconciliation	Spent time earlier as well as here, acknowledging Bill's concerns, "You're still really concerned about the impact of an outstanding sexual harassment claim on your job security." And asking, "What do you need to relieve your concerns?"	Keeping my judgment about the actual impact of this complaint on Bill's job in check and letting Bill know that his concerns have been heard, also that I as the mediator don't have the information about the impact of the complaint on his job.

Exhibit 6.1.

theory and practice, the professional is powerful, effective, competent, and resourceful.

Inventories

Reflection in action may seem impossible to manage given the tasks required of a mediator: observing the parties, tracking the patterns of their interaction, attending to their stories, considering possible strategies, and implementing practice techniques. When students complain that they cannot manage one more task, we ask them to remember the first few times they tried riding a bicycle— those tentative, awkward moments when they attempted to manage the multiple tasks of maintaining balance, pedaling, steering, braking, watching for traffic, and listening to a parent's instructions and exhortations to be careful. It may have seemed unlikely that it would ever be possible to put together the required tasks in order to ride the bicycle. It has been suggested that when the description of the program for riding a bicycle, the activities and their sequences, is written out, it extends to several hundred pages. Yet most of us learned to ride a bicycle, and skinned knees and bruised elbows were the only evidence of the struggle we faced.

Learning to reflect in the moment does not subject us to physical bruises, but for the beginner, developing the discipline of reflection is not without challenges and moments of awkwardness. To help mediators learn the practice and skill of reflection in action, we have created two inventories, or lists of questions that mediators can ask themselves before and after each mediation session.

Presession Inventory. The following questions focus attention on the activity of reflection; they help you become intentional about your use of the methods of reflective practice.

- What are the issues, the sources of the conflict, the barriers to and opportunities for resolution?

- How is this conflict similar to others in which I have intervened, and how is it different?

- What do I know about similar conflicts that will help me deal with this dispute and these disputants?

- What is different about me that will influence the way I approach the resolution of this conflict? What have I learned from other experiences that bears on this intervention?

- What approaches will be most helpful in dealing with this conflict? What skills and techniques will be most appropriate, effective, and responsive to the disputants and their way of dealing with their conflicts?

- What is my formulation? How can I explain the conflict situation and the parties' responses to the conflict and to one another?

- How will we (clients and mediator) know if we have succeeded?

By focusing attention on times in the mediation process when reflection in action can help mediators develop artistry, these questions provide a structure within which mediators can identify opportunities for learning—those surprising, unfamiliar events when professionals are faced with choices about strategy and technique. The questions can help mediators pay attention to those critical moments and honor their potential to enrich their understanding of their work. When mediators confront the unexpected events in practice, they are able to examine their customary responses to these moments and learn how their approach may be limiting their creativity and artistry. Schön (1983) refers to these moments as the opportunity to "surface the tacit understandings that have grown up around the repetitive experiences of a specialized practice" (p. 61). Noticing these moments provides opportunities to learn anew from each experience about the nature of practice, and to evaluate the effectiveness and relevance of the strategies, techniques, and skills used with clients.

Some mediators who have used this inventory have asked such questions as, Do I need to write down my answers? Is it necessary to answer every question? Should I use this inventory before every mediation? How do I know if my answers are correct? In response, we explain that the questions are tools to be used in whatever ways seem most helpful in attaining the goal of artistry. How the questions are used depends on what each person wants to gain from their application. Moreover, each person's learning process will differ. Some students see the questions as building intentionality, as giving them a mind-set that will lead to reflection in action. Others answer each question, because in doing so they deepen their knowledge about mediation practice or they create new ways of responding to the predictable events of a mediation. Still others use the questions as a method for developing discipline, as a continuing reminder of the importance of reflection in action.

Postsession Inventory. Using the following postsession inventory after a mediation session supports reflection on action. By answering these questions, mediators can examine their thoughts and actions, the patterns of their clients' behavior and their own responses, the consequences of their interventions for the clients and for the mediation process, and the choices their have made. The goals of the postsession inventory are the same as those of the presession inventory: to develop the habits of reflection, to maintain openness to new ways of understanding the behaviors of clients within the context of the conflict situation, to identify the choice points (critical moments) of the mediation, to evaluate the consequences of the judgments and decisions they have made, and to consider whether other approaches might have been constructive, appropriate, and effective.

- What was my initial formulation? In what ways was my formulation transformed as I engaged with the clients?
- Was I able to experiment? If so, what did I learn?

- Was my theoretical approach (constellation) helpful in deal-ing with the parties and the conflict?

- How was this conflict different from other, similar conflicts?

- Were my predictions about the dispute and the needs of the disputants accurate? If yes, in what way? If no, what did I miss?

- Were there surprises, unexpected responses, unanticipated issues, or curious or novel events? What brought them to my attention?

- How did I respond to those unexpected events?

- How did the clients respond to my strategies and approaches?

- How does what occurred affect my thinking about the dispute and the disputants?

- Was I able to reflect in action? If yes, when, with what result, and to what effect? If no, why not?

- How can I utilize the lessons from this experience in develop-ing my artistry, in learning new ways to assess the nature of the dispute, and in selecting appropriate and helpful interventions?

- What do I like about the way I handled the session or particu-lar interventions? What seemed artful, responsive, and effec-tive? Why?

- In what ways were my interventions unhelpful, unartful, or unresponsive?

- Could I have responded differently at any point in the mediation?

- What additional information or skill do I wish I had? How and where can I learn that?

We encourage you to use this inventory consistently and delib-erately for a period in order to understand the process of asking and responding to the questions. Repetitive use will develop the habit of reflection. Once you are familiar with the process and the results, you can then decide how best to employ the inventory in your practices. As with any tool, understanding the function, potential, and limitations of the inventory is essential to its appropriate use.

Coaching

In our discussion of artistry, particularly in Chapters Two and Three, we noted the importance of coaching in developing the habits of reflective practice. We presented extensive illustrations of the coaching methods we employ. Coaching serves two vital functions: it helps the mediator learn to use the methods of reflective practice, and it supports the mediator in developing the essential elements, the skills and knowledge, required for competent practice.

By being coached, mediators learn how to apply the methods of reflective practice, both during mediation sessions and afterward. By carefully and deliberately assisting mediators in identifying the surprises, the unexpected events, in a mediation, the coach assists them in examining their responses to the events and circumstances of the mediation interaction. With this guidance, mediators can assess the extent to which their interactions are either responsive to the unique circumstances of the session or shaped by resort to familiar responses. Coaching also helps mediators gain proficiency in developing and testing formulations, and in engaging in a deliberate process of experimentation.

Effective coaching helps mediators focus attention on key elements (critical moments) of the mediation, the choice points where they are faced with decisions about intervention strategies and techniques. With the assistance of the coach, mediators evaluate both the rationale for their actions and the impact on the parties and the overall mediation process. Understanding what interventions were constructive and why they were successful, as well as what approaches were unsuccessful and the reasons for these failures, helps mediators refine their analytical skills and improve their techniques.

Learning Journal

A learning journal is a way of systematically recording one's thoughts, impressions, concerns, questions, and reflections. It provides an opportunity for the mediator to express whatever comes to mind without searching for just the right word or worrying about spelling and grammar.

Why keep a learning journal? Keeping a learning journal frequently and regularly over months or years helps the mediator develop the habit of reflection, the discipline of critical analysis. The journal provides a picture of professional development; it depicts the changing nature of approaches to practice; it identifies the experiences, situations, readings, and other events that have shaped the mediator's understanding of his or her role and of the profession; and it serves as a repository for thoughts, questions, insights, observations, and reflections that arise in the course of practice. For some mediators, it can be a tool for analyzing and solving problems, while for others, the journal is a history of their professional development. Each mediator will discover his or her own unique purpose for keeping a learning journal.

The objectives of the learning journal are as follows:

- To help mediators reflect on their experiences
- To help them identify their strengths and weaknesses as well as their personal preferences, values, biases, and emotional reactions to various events
- To help mediators chart and evaluate their learning and development
- To facilitate mediators' integration of theory and practice
- To develop the habits and methods of a reflective practitioner

To keep a learning journal, purchase a notebook specifically for this purpose. Each entry should include the date, a brief description of the situation or learning event, a reflective comment about your learning, assumptions, insights, feelings, questions, and when possible, follow-up action, resources, or other to-do information.

A learning journal is personal and will reflect each person's personality, interests, and unique perspectives on practice. Be creative. Be honest. Be thorough. Challenge yourself.

It may be helpful to have others, particularly teachers and coaches but also peers, read your journal as part of their role in helping to further your studies and professional development.

Begin your learning journal by answering reflective questions. Here are some examples:

- What three things do I believe about conflict, about people in conflict, and about the value of the mediation process?
- What metaphors, images or expressions would I use to describe conflict?
- What is my pattern of behavior when involved in a conflict situation? With what aspects of that pattern am I comfortable or uncomfortable?
- What worries me most when I am involved in conflict?
- What would I most like to change about how I deal with conflict?
- What are three areas of mediation practice that I want to learn about?
- What strengths, knowledge, and skills do I bring to mediation? What are my limitations, the growing edges of my learning?

It might also be helpful to reflect on and include the following items in the learning journal:

- A critique of readings dealing with conflict, mediation, and conflict resolution

- Reactions to particular ideas or comments raised by others during discussions, peer supervision sessions, coaching, or courses
- Newspaper clippings about a current conflict and your analysis on how it was handled
- The recounting and analysis of a conflict in your personal or professional life—what worked for you, what did not, and why
- Any "brain waves" (new ideas, comments, insights) that may have occurred to you
- Perceptions about your values, biases, personal preferences, and conflict style

Reading

Reading infuses practice with new, provocative, curious, stimulating, and sometimes confusing concepts and approaches. Reading teaches theories, questions existing concepts, synthesizes ideas, and provides interpretations. The journey toward artistry is enhanced through reading. By gaining knowledge, evaluating your beliefs, and testing ideas in the laboratory of practice, you can develop a unique form of practice. Artists are not merely competent performers of a model they learned as novices, then refined through the apprentice and practitioner stages; they are talented interpreters of the profession, bringing their unique understanding of the field to the traditions of practice they have learned. Reading stimulates, provokes, challenges, informs, encourages, delights, arouses, and invigorates.

Shifting the Contract Between Mediator and Client

The activities and exercises described in this chapter teach the methods and provide opportunities to apply the principles of reflective practice. Without the mind-set of reflective practice, however, the methods are hollow practices, activities without focus and purpose. To become an artist and follow the path of reflective practice, mediators must also adopt the beliefs and values that underpin this approach to professional practice. The following list, adapted from Schön (1983), depicts some of the distinctions between a reflective practitioner and an expert. Schön describes the expert as a professional wedded to a model of practice that is grounded in the belief that an individual can acquire a body of knowledge that when applied to a problem set yields an effective and competent solution. Schön proposes that as practitioners develop the discipline of reflection in action, they will move from the model of the professional as expert to the model of the reflective practitioner.

Expert	*Reflective Practitioner*
It is presumed that I know, and I must claim that I do, regardless of my own uncertainty.	It is presumed that I know, but I am not the only one in the situation to have relevant and important knowledge. My uncertainties may be a source of learning for both me and my clients.
I keep my distance from the client and hold onto the expert's role. I give the client a sense of my expertise but convey a feeling of warmth and sympathy as a "sweetener."	I seek out connections to the client's thoughts and feelings. I allow her respect for my knowledge to emerge from her discovery of it in the situation.
I look for deference and status in the client's response to my professional persona.	I look for a sense of freedom and of real connection to the client, as a consequence of no longer needing to maintain a professional facade (Schön, 1983).

Mediators are generally schooled in other professions before entering the practice of mediation, and they bring to mediation the habits, values, and mind-sets of their profession of origin. Given the nature of much of the professional education provided in the North America, mediators will likely see themselves as experts, steeped in a specialized knowledge they bring to bear in helping clients solve instrumental problems. Schön suggests that the expert's self-worth is dependent on seeing himself or herself as confident, competent, and self-assured. There is no room for uncertainty, for exploration and discovery. The notion of learning from unanticipated events has no place in the temperament of the expert.

By contrast, the reflective practitioner acknowledges that disputants understand the conflict and its origins, dimensions, dangers, and opportunities better than anyone. The reflective practitioner is open to uncertainty, to exploring the unknown and the surprising, to seeking out information from clients, and to encouraging them to be active and engaged in the process. The reflective practitioner believes in the collaboration between mediator and disputants, and he trusts the clients to bring their knowledge and skill to bear on the problem. Committed to full, equal, and active partnership among the disputants and the mediator, the reflective practitioner actively seeks and relies on the expertise of the clients.

In practice, reflective practitioners are transparent, willing to reveal their thoughts, concerns, and ideas about the mediation process. As further evidence of the reflective practitioner's commitment to open and full consultation with clients, the artistic mediator does not hide behind the veil of professional detachment, like the physicians gathered at the foot of a bed in hushed conversation about the patient's status, prognosis, or treatment. Instead, the artistic mediator seeks clients' involvement, encouraging their questions, observations, and comments.

For the client as well, the relationship with a reflective practitioner is different from the experience with an expert:

Expert	*Reflective Practitioner*
I put myself into the professional's hands and, in	I join with the professional in making sense of my own case,

doing so, gain a sense of security based on faith.	and in doing so, gain a sense of increased involvement and action.
I have the comfort of being in good hands. I need only comply with the mediator's advice and all will be well.	I can exercise some control over the situation. I am not wholly dependent on the mediator; she is also dependent on information that only I can give and action that only I can take.
I am pleased to be served by the best person available.	I am pleased to be able to test my judgments about the mediator's competence. I enjoy the excitement of discovering her knowledge and the phenomena of her practice, and of learning about myself (Schön, 1983).

The client's relationships with the expert and the reflective practitioner are distinctively different from each other. In a relationship with a reflective practitioner, the client is invited, even encouraged, to become part of the delivery of professional services, to participate in all aspects of the process and in all decisions. This is a new role, different from the traditional delivery of professional services, in which the client seeks and obediently accepts (usually without question) the advice or treatment proposed by the expert. And because clients may be conditioned to the expert model of a professional relationship, the new relationship may be challenging for them, as well as for the mediator committed to the principles and methods of reflective practice. The lack of certitude and of the prescriptions or advice that distinguish the patient-client relationship and that offer the security of definite answers to problems may lead the client to lack confidence in the artistic mediator. However, uncertainty—the confusion created by a shift in the nature of the professional relationship—is an opportunity for the mediator to employ the reflective practice approach to help the client understand and appreciate this new role.

Walking the Path of Artistry

Think of a time when you were confronted by a situation in your mediation practice that was unexpected. You were surprised. Nothing in your training or experience provided a ready response. Yet you responded with an intervention, question, or approach that was unique or novel. Reflect on that experience and answer the following questions:

- What did you consider unique or surprising about the situation or experience?
- How did you become aware of the situation?
- What was your response to the surprising situation?
- What caused you to respond as you did?
- What information supported your decision?
- What was your thought process? What options did you weigh? What alternatives did you explore?
- On what did you reflect as you considered how to respond?

By using such questions to guide your exploration and by learning from your experiences through reflecting in action and reflecting on action, you can develop the discipline of reflection, and enhance your skills and knowledge.

Looking Back, Looking Forward

The journey toward artistry requires an ability to learn from experience. Understanding what approaches worked successfully and, most important, why they worked, yields critical knowledge that you can apply in subsequent situations. More than a collection of skills or habits, the process of reflection (whether in action or on action) is a matter of intention; it is a mind-set, a way of approaching the practice of your profession. Using the principles and practices described in this chapter will develop your ability to respond to the uncertain, surprising, and confounding events in a mediation. If you adopt the habits and methods we have presented, you will heighten your ability to respond flexibly, creatively, and with competence and effectiveness to those unusual situations.

In the following chapters we will describe in greater detail the nature of interactive process and how attention to this process leads, in combination with reflective practice, to artistry. Within the interactive process are a succession of critical moments. Choice points for the parties and the mediator. We explain how these critical moments play a key role in the development of artistry. And last, we discuss flow—the experience of being attentive to and engaged in the interactive moments of the mediation.

Part Three

Interactive Process

Chapter Seven

Combining the Elements of Interactive Process

The challenge for mediators at every session is reflected in the following scenario. The clients are coming in at 3:00 P.M. for a second session. The mediator has a basic understanding of the disputants' perceptions of the conflict, their positions on likely solutions, their flexibility in developing alternatives, and their legal posture. But what guides and informs the mediators' strategies and interventions once the mediation begins?

As they enter into the flow of the mediation, mediators and disputants engage in an evolving dialogue that characterizes and defines the mediation process. This reflexive dialogue is the *interaction*, the medium in which the mediation process is played out. This chapter describes interaction and examines its influence on the choices, responses, and decisions that mediators make throughout the process.

Interaction is the water in which people swim, the air we breathe, and in terms of mediation, the essential medium within which dialogue occurs. Mediators seldom look at the total interactional world separate from the people and action that takes place during the mediation, but interaction is the composite of everything that occurs. Mediators often take interaction for granted, as fish take the sea and birds take the air. There seems to be little reason to analyze interaction; it is constantly present and an integral aspect of the mediation process. In mediation, though, the choices mediators make in the course of a mediation are influenced by comments and questions from the other participants, by each person's interpretation of those comments and questions, and by each person's perceptions of the other people. The dialogue becomes the basis of the interaction, the medium in which mediators express their artistry, the place where skills, knowledge, and reflection merge. By not focusing on the essential elements and qualities of the interaction, a mediator can be oblivious to important dynamics that are critical to effectiveness and artistry.

Mediators cannot develop artistry in their practices without being fully aware of, sensitive to, and responsive to the interactions that occur during the mediation process. Artistry demands an enhanced level of understanding and finesse in dealing with mediation interaction.

Mediators who engage in the reflective work suggested in Part Two of this book will have identified and have access to the knowledge, beliefs, information, values, models, and theoretical understandings that form their unique constellations of theories. Their practices will be guided and informed by these elements in their constellations, and they will have developed an enhanced ability to create, assess, and evolve specific case formulations. To create formulations, however, mediators need the raw material, the information on which a formulation is based. The ingredients that give substance to formulations occur in the interaction. Mediators filter the interaction through their constellation of theories to understand and make sense of the conflict situation. They then apply what they know to the interaction through experiments, and thereby change the interaction. The reciprocal exchange involving mediators and disputants is the interactive process. (The process is represented graphically by the total area of intersection between mediator and disputants, as shown in Figure 7.1; the figure appears later in the chapter.)

Mediators are not passive purveyors of skills and techniques, but rather catalysts for change that takes place in the interaction. Mediators not only provide the crucible for heating up the interaction between the two clients, they are also in the crucible. Mediators are as much a dynamic part of the interaction as the disputants.

How mediators respond to and intervene with clients has an impact not only on the interactions between the disputants but also on the interactions between each disputant and the mediator. There are an infinite number of possibilities for interaction, because each exchange in the reflexive dialogue influences how others respond. Each moment, each comment or question, shapes the next. Experienced mediators know that no set of disputants, even those with seemingly identical issues and situations, responds the same way as any other set of disputants to their conflict and to the intervention of the mediator. Experienced mediators also know that they themselves respond differently to disputants in separate situations whose conflict dynamics appear similar. It is this factor that makes mediation a creative process. There is no blueprint, no script, no formula that can account for the variations in how people respond to one another in the course of the interactions in mediation. Mediators can respond to a moment only in that moment.

As noted in earlier chapters, mediators who aspire to artistry in their practices approach outwardly similar situations in very different ways, on the basis of their formulation of the case, their unique constellation of theories, and the level of reflection they are using to integrate these theories into their practice. There is no single way to mediate artistically; there is no recipe, formula, or special technique that will work perfectly in every situation. The river that is the flow of the mediation is never the same twice.

The best analogy for the immediacy and responsiveness required in artistic mediation interaction is jazz music or improvisational acting. These art forms that cannot be entirely planned require consummate skill, experience, and knowledge; they rely on the artist to add nuances, shades of understanding, and sudden awareness. Jazz musicians may play the same basic piece of music gig after gig, yet the performance will be different each time, as a result of the interaction among the musicians. The actor may rely on a basic story line and may have played a role more than once, but the quality of each presentation will be shaped by the interaction among the performers. Each musician or actor listens and responds to every other performer; each influences the others in a reciprocal manner, so that the resulting performance is unique and the product of their interactions. How they experience and react to one another in the moment determines the course of the performance. Their delivery of the performance is based not merely on the skills and talents of the individual performers, but also on their ability to interact with and respond to one another. So, too, for the artistic mediator. The quality of the mediation process is determined in part by the skill and knowledge of the mediator, and in part by the mediator's ability to attend to and be responsive to the interactions between the mediator and the disputants.

Disputants who seemed prepared to conclude their discussions on economic issues in their contract dispute suddenly turned their attention to less tangible concerns, such as previously unresolved conflicts that had eroded their ability to trust one another. The mediator asked how they would know when their agreement had been fulfilled, and that question stimulated the discussion about trust. What caused this shift is the interactive quality of the mediation process. A question typically asked by mediators as disputants are finalizing their agreements stimulated discussion of a concern that seemingly was unrelated to the substantive matter under consideration. One person's response to the question shifted attention from one issue to another. The interaction altered the course of the mediation. A different client might have reacted differently to the mediator's question. A different mediator may not have asked the question in that form, at that time, or at all. To be effective and resourceful, mediators must practice in the eternal now, in the interplay of interactive moments.

Defining Interaction

Mediation interaction is unique, ephemeral, spontaneous, reciprocal, and synergistic. In these interactive moments, mediators manifest their artistry. Most mediators, particularly those at the novice and apprentice stages of development, focus their attention primarily on the content issues being mediated. More experienced mediators also focus on the process dynamics between and among the participants and the mediator. They understand that the mediation interaction includes not only the substantive issues of the dispute, but also the process dynamics. Interaction in mediation is the combination of the communications, thoughts, feelings, intentions, interpretations, and behaviors of each person, which can and do affect the experiences and reactions of the other participants. It includes the internal and hidden processes as well as the external, observable communications and behaviors. Interaction includes all that is directly and indirectly communicated.

Figure 7.1 shows two intersecting circles, each representing a participant, and a third intersecting circle representing the mediator. This is a pictorial representation of the total area of interaction available to analyze. The interactional system of the two participants is changed by the presence of the third party, the mediator. One of the truths of mediation interaction is that by being a part of

Figure 7.1. Interaction in Mediation.

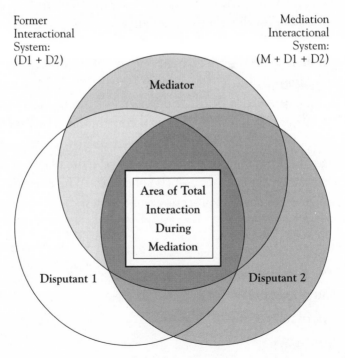

Former
Interactional
System:
(D1 + D2)

Mediation
Interactional
System:
(M + D1 + D2)

Mediator

Area of Total
Interaction
During
Mediation

Disputant 1

Disputant 2

the interactional system, mediators act as change agents. They change the participants' former interactional system just by being present, as witnesses even if not as intervenors. In physics, scientists have learned that merely observing a nuclear experiment changes the outcome of the experiment. "This world of relationships is rich and complex. . . . With relationships we give up predictability for potentials. . . . None of us exists independent of our relationships with others. Different settings and people evoke some qualities from us and leave others dormant. In each of these relationships, we are different, new in some way" (Wheatley, 1992, p. 34). Mediators should view the mediation process as creating a temporary interactional system in which each person influences and in turn is influenced by the others.

Elements of Mediation Interaction

The elements of interaction exist in all mediation efforts; they are universal to the process of mediation interaction. Although for purposes of description the elements of interaction are separated, during mediation sessions these elements are not discrete and separate but interconnected, acting in that total area of interaction simultaneously.

The exact qualities of these elements of interaction are not fixed but rather moving points along a continuum. The quality of a mediator's interaction is "fuzzy," as described by Kosko (1993), meaning that the mediator can be measured to a greater or lesser degree on a scale for each one of the elements. The essential elements of the interactional process are as follows:

- Relationship
- Power and conflict orientation
- Communication
- Range of interaction
- Transparency

- Respectfulness
- Balance and neutrality
- Climate
- Modeling

Taken together, these elements are the gestalt of the mediation interaction.

The first three qualities—relationship, power, and communication—are criteria that pertain equally to the disputants and the mediator. Mediators need to be attentive to the interactions among all parties, including their own interactions with the disputants, in order to assess and respond accurately to these three elements. The other elements in the list are shaped primarily by the mediator's actions that affect the interaction in the room.

All of the elements of interaction are inherent in all mediation processes, regardless of the nature of the conflict, the mediator's formulation, or the model of mediation employed. A model of mediation may give mediators some guidance as to what are the ideal qualities of these elements—the benchmarks of good enough or ideal practice from that model's perspective. Yet across models, mediators must address these elements of interaction during the mediation. When these elements are present at appropriate levels and in balance with one another, the mediation interaction will be rich, robust, productive, and artistic.

Relationship

Participants in mediation have relationships that may be either rich with history or spare. They have developed some patterns of behavior based in part on their experiences and in part on their perceptions of one another. They come to mediation with aspirations and fears about the current and future state of their relationship. Divorcing spouses often have years of intimate relationship that affect their interaction. They may have experienced the use of tactics of manipulation or intimidation that limit their willingness to trust one another, or they may have developed the ability to work cooperatively. Parties in workplaces may have limited or extensive histories of workplace relationships. All mediation participants will bring to the mediation the qualities and entrenched patterns of their preexisting relationships. If participants have a very thin and remote premediation relationship, they interact more like strangers; they do not have well-formed patterns of interaction and do not fully understand each other's attributions, ideas, and prejudices. A full and established relationship is often absent in community mediation, where neighbors may have had limited contact until the dispute emerged and will probably have little contact following the mediation. The quality of the disputants' preexisting relationship and their need or desire to interact successfully after their dispute is resolved are crucial factors in determining the level of their investment in the temporary mediation relationship.

Because disputants have a preexisting relationship, they have already developed an orientation of dealing with conflict ranging from avoidance to opposition. This orientation is produced not only by each disputant's personal response to conflict but also by the combination of their individual responses. An individual may generally employ an avoidance approach to conflict, yet find in the unfolding of a workplace conflict that their strategy has shifted toward a competitive response as a result of the interaction with the other disputant. For example, in a neighborhood dispute a businesswoman known for her shrewd deals may approach the mediation with her customary competitive orientation. The neighbor's customary response is to avoid conflict and he approaches the mediation with that orientation. If the parties have had previous encounters, they may have established a pattern for dealing with each other and may anticipate how the other is likely to behave in the mediation. Yet even though the disputants may have established patterns for handling their conflicts, these patterns will be modified during the interaction in mediation, simply because of the mediator's presence. The relationship between the disputants is thus altered by the involvement of the mediator.

Mediators usually have a superficial, role-defined relationship with disputants. Over time, during the mediation session, the mediator develops a working relationship with each party as well as with the parties as a couple or a group (such as divorcing spouses, business partners, or employees in the same company). As a result of these ongoing relationships, the mediator and the disputants will experience shifts in their interactions. Mediators often refer to this as their rapport with clients, which is one factor in the interactional area of relationship.

Another aspect of the relationship element is the possibility of very strong power differentials in disputants' relationships outside the mediation, such as between bosses and employees, parents and children, and spouses. The dynamic of power may create a unique set of relationships during the mediation, or a "mediation culture" of interaction. Relationships during the mediation may appear more egalitarian than they were either before or following the mediation. Sometimes the temporary, interactional nature of the mediation relationship changes the power dynamics of the disputants' current and future relationship, and the mediator is intentional and artful in managing these power dynamics of relationship during interaction.

Mediators are sometimes selected to mediate because they have deep, ongoing relationships with the disputants, such as pastors acting as mediators for their parishioners. In their other roles, the mediators may have developed trust and predictability, which contribute to their ability to gain a constructive relationship during the temporary, three-way interaction during mediation. At other times mediators are interacting with parties who are unknown to them. Their credibility as third-party neutrals often depends on past performance, reputation, and lack of a prior relationship with the disputants. These factors contribute to the perception of the mediator as neutral and unbiased. Mediators in North America (as distinct from other cultures) are often selected to mediate because they have no prior knowledge of the participants, and because of that lack of relationship they are perceived as more neutral and unbiased.

The nature and degree of preexisting relationships between the participants or with the mediator will determine the nature and significance of the patterns of interaction during mediation. They may be either complementary, conflicting, symmetrical, or distinct. Complementary patterns of interaction use cues from the others in the interaction to provide a similarity of response that seems to add onto the last exchange, to complement it. Conflicting interaction is useful for surfacing differences, whereas complementary patterns establish what is mutual. Symmetrical patterns of interaction are useful for maintaining the balance between disputants because what you do to one you must do to the other. Distinct patterns of interaction rely on the fact that the parties are different and must be responded to differently during the interaction rather than scrupulously the same as the other party. People who have thick, rich relationships have developed one or more of these relationship patterns over time. Strangers, who lack this history, have a more limited ability to understand one another, and their anxiety about engaging in a mediation is heightened because the interactions are unpredictable. So they must build one or more of these interactional patterns during the mediation process; it then becomes part of the relationship factors.

Most models of mediation urge mediators to develop at least a minimum level of relationship, to express empathy and build rapport. Counselors and other helping professionals need to develop trusting relationships with their clients. The extent of these relationships is determined by their function. Although counselors and therapists may spend several sessions developing sufficient trust to engage their clients, because of the nature and focus of their professional work, mediators do not need to develop the same depth of trust in their relationships with clients. However, mediators will develop patterns of relationship that contribute or hinder artistry in interaction.

In mediation, the disputants and the mediator should be able to maintain a quality of relationship that is sufficient to accomplish the disputants' goals. Following are reflective questions you may want to ask yourself about this aspect of interaction:

- What is the history of the disputants' relationship, and if relevant, what is the history of your relationship with them?
- How intimate or formal, close or distant have the clients been in the past? How about now?
- What would they like their relationship to be when they end mediation?
- What qualities of relationship do they and you value?
- Do you have expectations and values about professional relationships with clients?

Power

Power is an important element in shaping the mediation interaction. For many people, power holds a negative connotation, because it is perceived as *power over*, the imposition of one person's will on the behavior of another. From the mid-1890s to the early part of this century, both Georg Simmel ([1950]) and Max Weber ([1978]; cited in Lukes, 1986) described power in terms of domination and submission. In what he called his concept of reciprocal effectiveness, Simmel elaborated by explaining that those who are influenced also have an influence on those who try to dominate. In his view, those who seek and use power to exert control are themselves controlled by the subject of their own behavior. Any parent who has tried to get children to clean up their rooms understands that their power over their children is influenced by the children's reaction to the exercise of power. Any mediator who has experienced a power struggle with a client during mediation also knows that the one who is asserting power can be influenced by the reaction of the party they are attempting to control. Controlling behaviors are successful only if the person who is being controlled is in fact controlled by it.

Bertrand Russell ([1938]; cited in Lukes, 1986) explains power in a different way; he declares that "power is the production of intended effects" (p. 19). Although many people might want to have power over the weather, they are not rainmakers and therefore cannot produce the intended effect of having it rain at their will, so they have no power over the weather. Power, according to Russell, comes in three forms: as direct physical power over the body, as rewards or inducements, or as influence on opinions. This three-part definition is very similar to a concept proposed by John Kenneth Galbraith ([1983]; cited in Lukes, 1986), who describes *condign power* (threat of punishment), *compensatory power* (reward used to promote certain behavior), and *conditioned power* (the use of beliefs to influence behavior indirectly).

Kenneth Boulding (1989) sees power as the ability to get what one wants, but he too believes that power appears and may be exerted in three forms: *destructive*, *productive*, or *integrative*. He describes the methods for obtaining power as the use of threat, exchange, or love, or power over, power through, and power with. Rummel ([1984], 1991) defines power by stating that there are *nonsocial powers* (such as identitive, assertive, physical power, and force), and *social powers* (such as coercive, bargaining, authoritative, intellectual, altruistic, and manipulative powers).

Using these definitions of power can help mediators understand and then develop appropriate responses to the dimension and applications of power during the mediation interaction. Mediators do not have the power to produce the hoped-for effects of cooperation between disputing neighbors or arguing spouses, but the disputants themselves do have and can assert that power, if they have that intention. A mediator may have social power over disputants, by virtue of professional status, title, position, and the ability to charge a fee, yet the application of social power may be influenced by the disputants. A mediator cannot use physical force over disputants' bodies, yet he can have a direct influence over the character, focus, and form of their interactions.

· Mediators possess and often use their personal power as professional knowledge and skill, linguistic ability, and authority in the role of mediator in constructive ways. If they fail to use these sources of potentially constructive power, they may feel and appear powerless, and they might decide to employ manipulative, coercive, power-over methods, turning into what has been called by Folberg and Taylor (1984) a "muscle mediator."

Considering that each person in the mediation has his or her own unique set of personal and social powers, it does seem as if Rummel's (1991) definition of noncoercive conflict resolution methods as powers meeting and balancing holds true. Ultimately, Boulding's assessment seems to be the most helpful in thinking about power during mediation interaction, because the use of personal and social power in these situations contributes to either a favorable or an unfavorable end, depending on whether the power is employed for destructive, productive, or integrative purposes. If overall the powers used by the disputants and the mediator are constructive or integrative, they can be said to have utilized the power in the room wisely.

Obviously the disputants and the mediator should not use physical power, bribery, threat, or other coercive powers as methods to achieve results. The end does not justify the means. The value of the interactive experience should not be sacrificed to the blind insistence on reaching a particular goal at any cost and by any method. The interactive qualities can be destroyed by a headlong rush into outcomes that do not honor the principles of proper interaction. Many mediators hold that manipulation, while possibly effective in producing an outcome, is not ethical. As Haynes (1989) and Bush and Folger (1994) assert, mediators have a responsibility to engage in active intervention, to use their forms of power in the service of the disputants' objectives, and when possible, to foster the parties' empowerment. Mediators must therefore find an appropriate balance of power during the interaction.

One simple, well-known, and frequently exercised method employed by mediators in asserting their power to shape the interaction is to work with the disputants to establish and then enforce ground rules. Mediators who do this are in effect changing the interaction between disputants by changing their "conflict culture" and helping set expectations for the interaction during the mediation session. The methods for establishing these ground rules will vary depending on the mediator's orientation or model, yet setting such rules has an impact on the interaction. We propose that a mediator who does not believe that a "mediator knows best" might want to assess whether their interactions and rule setting, their power-over behavior during a session, is pointing to a discontinuity between their theories, their formulations, and the interactive process. Unless these three are aligned, artistry will not be possible.

Disputants and mediators should understand their sources of power, their methods for applying power, and the impact of their power on others, and they should be able to use their power in a constructive or integrative manner during mediation interaction.

Following are some reflective questions to ask about power as an element of interaction:

- What are the sources and forms of a mediator's power, and how is power used?
- How do they and you perceive their own, your own, and the other disputant's power?
- How are these perceptions supporting or limiting their and your ability to proceed?
- Do they and you have available the full range of responses, or are they or you operating out of conditioned responses?
- Are they or you making concessions as appeasement or to placate the other?
- Are they or you dominating the interaction?

Communication

Communication is by its very nature interactive. What one person say affects the other, and what is not said also has an impact. Fostering communication creates interaction, and interaction creates the need for communication. So when disputants start a mediation by stating the equivalent of "What we have here is a failure to communicate," they are also implying that "What we have here is a failure in our interaction." Helping disputants create mechanisms and opportunities to interact may be more far-reaching than merely training disputants in the use of "I statements" or other communication devices or techniques.

Communication content and process can have great power, if power is seen as the ability to produce intended effects. Mediators who want to act more artistically in the realm of interaction needs to ask themselves the following questions about the element of communication interaction between the disputants:

- How masked or clear is the communication?
- How direct or indirect is the communication?
- Do the parties have preferred methods or modes of communication? Does the mediator? Are there conflicts with respect to these modes?
- How easy is it to communicate with the disputants?
- What is the overall pattern of communication between the disputants and between each disputant and the mediator?
- How much of the communication is about self, the other, or the context?

Communication that is clear, constructive, and direct contributes to better interaction during the mediation. We believe this is true because it is culturally consistent and because it reduces ambiguity. Other cultures value different modes of communication.

Culture shapes the nature, form, purpose, and language of communication. When mediating with people from cultures that value other communication qualities, mediators should consider what forms of communication will best serve the disputants and the mediation process.

Mediators must be sensitive to the subtle qualities of communication. There are great individual differences in nature, quality, and style of communication. Some disputants speak freely, candidly, and with ease, while others are more hesitant and seemingly less willing to reveal information. Mediators should also attend to possible differences in the manner in which disputants communicate with one another and with them. For example, when one party is reluctant to talk and is less engaged in the interaction, the mediator may interpret this behavior as evidence that the topic is too sensitive, that the party is feeling vulnerable, or that the other party is acting in an intimidating manner. Testing these possible formulations through a carefully constructed set of experiments will reveal which if any of these formulations is accurate; the mediator can then design an appropriate strategy or intervention. To address these concerns about the quality of the communication, mediators should pay attention to the overall communication pattern between the disputants and between them and the mediator.

Virginia Satir (1972) believed that all communication sent and received has three components: it says something about the self, something about the other, and something about the context in which the communication is embedded. Sometimes in mediation, instead of focusing on the content of the messages, the mediator needs to refocus attention on the context that seems to be implied in the person's message. The mediator should try to understand whether the disputant is implying that he or she is in a context in which he or she must be careful or in which it is not safe to say what he or she believes for fear of retribution. The mediator might want to note whether the context requires seriousness yet the messages seem frivolous. Another area of possible inquiry is the extent to which the communication has relevance only for individuals or for the entire system.

Other questions that the disputants' patterns of communication might prompt include, Are they posturing, saving face, or making minor concessions without caving in? What does their communication say about their view of themselves and the person to whom they are talking? Does the language or tone imply disregard and cynicism? Do their statements seem authentic and genuine? Mediators can learn the answers to the questions only if they metaphorically step away from the interaction for a moment to see the communication from a different vantage point. They can then decide whether to alter their strategy, continue with the current approach, or offer their insights about the communication patterns to the disputants. If mediators do not obtain this long-range perspective on communication by watching for patterns and functionality (or what purpose the communication serves for the interaction), they will not be able to develop strategies that either change or support the interaction. Watching for patterns and the effects of communication in the interactional realm leads to a greater understanding of the process.

Effective communication during interaction is achieved when sufficient rapport among the parties is maintained and when adequate feedback loops are established. The goal for the mediator is to ensure that information is clearly sent and correctly received, and that the method of communication is constructive and not self-defeating. Additional reflective questions about the element of communication in interaction include the following:

- What is the "meta-message" of their and your communication?

- How flowing or hesitant, formal or informal is it?

- What is self-defeating about their or your communication style? What could improve it?

- What are the patterns that they and you use? Should they be changed?
- How do blockages occur, and how do they and you handle them?

Range of Interaction

The quality of interaction can be measured in terms of the range of freedom and self-expression experienced by the disputants and the mediator. When the interaction is effective and positive, each person has a full range of interaction in that they can express themselves to their own level of comfort. The range of behavior and expression will understandably change over the course of the mediation, so the ideal range is not a target, a specific and quantifiable amount, but rather is experienced over the course of the mediation. A full range of interaction means the full range of expression. Sometimes the disputants are still, sometimes they are animated, and other times they are reflective.

The range of interaction can be expressed as a continuum with the words *constricted* and *full* at either end. For example, a disputant who is actively engaged during the start of a mediation session but grows increasingly quiet and uncommunicative could reflect either a difficulty with communication or a restriction of the range of interaction. Clearly the disputant is not being an active participant. The challenge for the mediator is to discover the underlying reason for the behavior. The cause might be as simple as preoccupation about an unrelated matter, or the behavior might signal an experience of being unheard, unattended to, or disempowered. A restricted range of interaction, no matter what the cause, should mobilize the artistic mediator to probe further until the range is again full. A constricted range of interaction by anyone is a concern.

In addition to concern about the disputants' range of interaction is concern that the mediator have a similarly extended or constricted range. When disputants and mediators are unable to participate fully and effectively—if their ranges of interaction with each other seem restricted, rigid, or curtailed—the mediator must search for and understand the underlying cause. The source may be external to the interaction, such as injunctions from attorneys or others to keep silent and make no decisions, or it may be in the character of the interaction, such as resulting from miscommunication or an unintended slight, or more insidiously, from a calculated effort to minimize or discredit. There may be reasons for participants to fear retribution for candidly expressing their views. If the mediator senses that the range of interaction is constrained—for example, if a disputant is intimidated when the other party expresses anger in a forceful manner—the mediator may need to limit the range of interaction in the expression of anger during the session in order to ensure a range of interaction in other areas.

When the interactive process is going well and all participants experience the full range of their interaction, they appear and feel relaxed, they are able to smile and use humor, and their full range of self (intellectual and emotional) is available. The breadth and range of the interaction depends on the mediator's model and the context of the dispute. Some models limit the full range of interaction between disputants. For example, some mediators do not discuss feelings or allow discussion about past hurts as part of the mediation because their model states that this is counterproductive or outside the range of mediation practice. Some mediators believe that allowing disputants to talk about their feelings is practicing therapy, so they do not facilitate or allow the expression of the range of feelings or emotions. If the mediator's model, approach, or constellation of theories supports a full exploration of past as well as current concerns, and if it says that it is legitimate to facilitate feelings, it would be fair to expect to see the full scope of interaction manifested in the mediator's interaction. If the mediator does not think that mediators in this type of conflict should get into the emotional dimension, the mediator will have a shortened range of interaction with the clients and will limit emotions during the session. This reduced range may be very appropriate to the type of dispute, the parties, and the context (such as court-connected with a short time), but it will inhibit the full range of expression.

In assessing the range of interaction, mediators observe whether the participants seem free to have a full range of feelings, and whether they themselves are free to respond in multiple ways or seem constrained. To be fully aware of the range of interaction requires that mediators first learn to identify the possible range for the types of disputes they mediate. With that knowledge they are then able to function fully and completely within that range and to become aware when that range seems full and open or when it seems restricted. Having this information and being attentive to the quality of the interaction allows the mediator to intervene when the range of interaction is inappropriately constrained.

Questions that mediators might ask themselves about the range of interaction during mediation sessions include the following:

- Do you have an ideal picture of the range of interaction for the disputes you mediate? Does the range become larger or smaller depending on the nature of the dispute, the context, or the attitude of the disputants?
- What factors would lead you to restrict or expand the range of interaction?
- Are there boundaries that the mediator dare not cross?
- Are the disputants and the mediator free to explore all aspects of the problem?
- If the disputants really needed some clarifying information, would the mediator be able to provide it?
- Is the mediator and are the disputants able to express emotions?
- Are there realms of information that cannot be brought into mediation?
- Are there external conditions affecting the range of interaction?

Transparency

Transparency in mediation interaction means that there is nothing hidden, mystical, or magical about the process and interaction. Transparency in practice is an element of reflective practice, as noted in Chapter Six in the discussion of the distinction between the reflective practitioner and the expert. Reflective practitioners openly discuss their process with disputants and engage disputants in decisions that affect the process and interaction.

The effect of interaction during mediation can certainly seem magical, such as when two disputants who had great dislike and disrespect for each other turn cooperative and civil. It can certainly be a remarkable moment when formerly hostile parties provide each other with recognition and apologies, and when grown men cry openly and women show their deep inner strength. Yet these extraordinary moments in interaction are brought about not by making use of hidden or manipulative tricks, or by applying secret skills, but by the very nature of the open interaction that occurs between the disputants and between the disputants and the mediator. By being honest in their interactive process, mediators inspire honesty between the disputants and with the mediator.

Mediation interactions must support this premise, by being open and subject to scrutiny at all times. If a client inquires about an intervention, question, or comment, mediators should respond honestly, candidly, and openly. Not only does such a response engender increased confidence in the mediator and the process, it also models behavior that the disputants may follow. Moreover, when mediators have access to their constellations of theories and the formulations derived from these theories, they are able to respond to such questions from disputants; they know what they are doing and why. If mediators are practicing with intention, they know, moment to moment, what interventions they have selected, how those interventions relate to their formulation, and the basis in their constellation of theories for the development of that formulation. In this way there should be no mystery as to why and what and how mediators interact with disputants.

Transparency in interaction also means that mediators may ask disputants to take a risk by playing their cards or stating their true intentions, credibility, and capabilities. As with the other elements of interaction, transparency is not an absolute; there are gradations and variations. There is no expectation that each person will reveal all they are thinking and feeling simply because another person asks a question. However, to the extent that the disputants and the mediator are willing to respond candidly to one another, the level of transparency is heightened and the quality of the interaction is enhanced. For example, if the mediator senses that anyone is keeping a secret, the system is not transparent. If the interaction seems cloudy, unclear, or unexplained, it is important to slow it down to allow the person who is confused to ask questions. Disputants who have hidden agendas often cannot do transparent process; they get caught at a certain point or refuse to answer. Hidden agendas or positions can become land mines in interaction, unless skillfully handled and openly dealt with by the mediator. Again, using the interaction as the key, the mediator can simply note what seems confusing or unclear or what could be taken for a manipulation and see how that reflection of lack of transparency changes the interaction.

Process precedes content. If the mediator wants honest content, he or she must mirror and set the stage for it by doing honest process and interaction. When this happens, we have found, not only do mediators feel better because they have been assured that they did nothing that was unsupported by ethics, standards, and good practice, but also this level of transparency often leads to a better climate and ultimately to firmer, longer-lasting agreements.

Our aspiration for the reader is that your interactions toward and among the disputants should be open, able to be explained and talked about, and at all times come from a place of honesty. The questions you could ask yourself to determine if the element of transparency is present in interaction are as follows:

- Does everyone in the session understand what they are attempting to do, and why?
- Are the rules or guidelines of behavior explicit?
- Is someone expecting the mediator to work magic to reduce the tension or bring about the resolution?
- Does anyone feel manipulated or unduly persuaded?
- Does the interaction seem forced or natural?

Respectfulness

Civility, generally expressed in ground rules developed in the early phase of mediation, is encouraged in the hope of leading to better interaction. Identifying behaviors that promote a sound process as well as those that likely interfere with effective mediation sets the stage for constructive interaction. The range of behaviors tolerated, encouraged, or prescribed can be broad or narrow, depending on many factors, including the nature of the dispute and the wishes of the disputants and the mediator. Each person may have a different threshold for what is considered respectful treatment, and these values or expectations may be culturally determined. Because disputants and mediators carry into the mediation session their own views about respectful and disrespectful treatment, it is often helpful in interaction to make these assumptions explicit, not only in the early, rule-setting stages of mediation but also consistently throughout the session.

Even when there are no violations of the overt mediation rules or guidelines for disputant behavior, sometimes tone of voice, body posture, and other mannerisms can convey disrespect. Attention to these less overt displays of disrespect is essential for mediators who want to ensure that the interactions are not compromised.

One of the hallmarks of respectful treatment during a session is the honoring of a contrary position. When parties can openly disagree, without having to sanitize their views, this is respectful interaction, and it conveys the principle of genuineness and empowerment. By their behavior mediators can model an appropriately open, curious, and nonjudgmental approach to the expression of contrary positions.

If mediators (or disputants) detect an action, comment, or behavior that seems disrespectful, they should thoughtfully and appropriately identify the incident, calling attention to the offending behavior. By stopping the interaction and focusing on the disrespectful incident, the mediator heightens the moment, allowing the event of disrespect to be discussed as part of the interaction. Since one of the goals of interaction is clear and open process, by naming the error the mediator both models transparency and provides an opportunity for the disputants to decide whether and how they will deal with the situation. If mediators continue as if the disrespectful words or behavior had not occurred, they deny reality, which is in itself disrespectful. By failing to note the incident of disrespect, mediators implicitly condone the behavior.

Encouraging respectful behavior does not suggest the need to be overly scrupulous or to have the sense of walking on eggshells for fear that the disputants or the mediator might offend the other participants. The mediator's goal should be to instill the process with a concern for and attention to respectful interaction, not to set a rigid and impossible standard of behavior. The pervasive tone of respectfulness is often brought to and maintained in the mediation by the mediator's attention to and awareness of this element of interaction. Disrespect is harmful; respect supports effective communication. At a minimum, mediators should not allow harm to occur in mediation.

Complaining is acceptable, but contempt is disrespectful. John Gottman (1993) has noted in his work with couples that valid and normal complaints can become the "negative cascade" of feelings that move into more and more disrespect through usual stages, including the turning of complaints into personalized contempt, which result in the turning away, stonewalling, or ignoring of the person. The complaints may well be valid, but by turning them into contempt and stonewalling behavior, the person is showing a level of disrespect of the other party. Janet Johnston and Vivienne Roseby (1997) have noted this same factor of disrespect in divorcing families, who project negative attributions on each other as "vilification of the other," resulting in high levels of conflict behavior that often lead to major social and psychological problems for the disputants and the children caught in the conflict. If the mediator is trying to interact with a disputant who cannot ever respect the other party, even when that person is acting respectfully, there is some question as to whether mediation efforts will be effective in creating the type of interaction that promotes dialogue and ultimately produces mediated agreements. The end does not justify the means; a set of mediated agreements that leaves one or both disputants feeling disrespected is not worth the process.

When disputants have difficulty showing respect to one another, when angry words turn into hostility, or when civil discourse is difficult to sustain, the cause may be unresolved frustrations, anxiety about the impact of the conflict, anger and disappointment, or feelings of righteousness. Whatever the source, the underlying message communicated from one party to the other is, "How dare you!" When the indignancy between the parties demonstrates this stuck interactional pattern, the interaction is no longer productive for content resolution. To restore a modicum of civility, mediators must turn their attention to the disrespectful behaviors as well as to the underlying causes; otherwise the mediation process will be compromised.

In the mediation of a postdivorce conflict about parenting concerns, the mother, a Hispanic woman, insisted on referring to her former spouse and the father of her child as Mr. Jones, despite an agreement between the parties, and the mediator's encouragement, that they would use first names. For the mother, the use of the more formal term in referring to her ex-husband was not simply a matter of conformity with the couple's customs or linguistic formality (which occurs in languages that have formal and informal syntax). Rather, it was her way of distancing and disrespecting her former spouse, through an exaggerated, stylized, and scrupulously proper demonstration of respect and formality that had the effect of making her former husband less important and more remote. He took offense at her behavior, experiencing it as disrespect even though she pretended to be acting respectfully. In response, and to protect a measure of trust and respect in the interaction, the mediator called attention to the issue of respectful treatment, both because of the parties' agreement regarding respect and because the interaction would otherwise suffer. By bringing the issue of respect, and in particular the use of the former husband's formal name, to their attention as part of the interaction, the mediator facilitated a discussion that led to acknowledgment of the behavior and reconfirmation of their agreement concerning respectful treatment of one another.

Interaction is enhanced and the disputants' opportunity to engage in a constructive process is safeguarded when there is both an expectation and an experience of civil treatment. Respectful behavior supports each person's opportunity to express his or her thoughts and feelings fully, to take contrary positions, and to participate fully and with dignity in the interaction.

When mediators are assessing the element of respectfulness in their mediation interactions, they may want to ask themselves the following questions:

- What are my own expectations regarding respect and civil discourse?
- In what ways do cultural variations, practices, and customs influence my thinking about the nature of a respectful interaction?
- Is it possible to disagree without being disagreeable?
- Does anyone feel shunned, left out, or unattended?
- Is anyone feeling so attacked that they have put up barriers and are maintaining a defensive manner?
- Are the parties able to show their true feelings without fear of being shut down by the other?

- Are they able to maintain a personal distance from each other that still allows enough interaction?

Balance and Neutrality

If mediation interaction is working well, then each person has the experience of being allowed enough time, enough opportunity to speak, enough support, and enough encouragement so that the process seems balanced for each participant. The mediator is ultimately responsible for maintaining a proper balance in interaction between the parties by noting when balance exists or pointing out when it does not, by establishing a structure and form that nurtures balance, and at times by the judicious use of certain interventions. When imbalance occurs, it may signal that the balance between the participants is naturally skewed—that one person has more information, a stronger sense of power, a more expansive sense of the possible options for settlement, a more congenial communication or negotiation style, or a lower anger threshold or less natural defensiveness in dealing with conflict. Without creating unhealthy alliances or alignments, mediators should attend to possible imbalances in any of these areas, call the imbalance to the disputants' attention, and when appropriate, intervene.

Some models of mediation rely on the conversational structure of the interaction to encourage and protect balance. Providing equal air time, spending equivalent time with each disputant during caucuses, being sure to ask a question of the second party after asking a question of the first, and in general behaving toward the parties in scrupulously equal ways are methods routinely used by mediators who hope to ensure balance in the interaction. There are innumerable other approaches that may be used to achieve balance in interaction.

Mediators who adopt a more active and interventionist approach to the matter of balance in mediation may utilize techniques such as active power balancing, using voice-over, which allows the mediator to reinterpret what one party said, similar to the way a foreign film can be dubbed with language the viewer can understand. Paraphrasing can be used to assist less articulate disputants. The goal is not equality but equity, not a perfect division but a balance. Achieving this equilibrium is not always exactly like an algebraic equation where an operation to one side is repeated on the other, although for some cases a scrupulous structural balance must be maintained.

Furthermore, what each party needs in order to experience the interaction as balanced is peculiar to that individual. For one person, balance occurs only when each party has equal time to speak, while for the other person the amount of air time is irrelevant. Mediators must not only take into account their own sense of what constitutes balance, but they must also consider the particular concerns of the disputants.

Neutrality is a distinct concept that requires a disinterested stance in regard to the outcome but may involve the mediator taking an active role in nurturing balance between the disputants. Mediators may experience competing demands regarding neutrality. On the one hand, they are encouraged to provide equal treatment, while on the other hand they are castigated if they fail to support the less powerful party. Because of the range of mediation forms and contexts, the field itself often gives mediators contradictory ethical demands. There are a number of good articles on the topic of neutrality in the literature that can help mediators who may be struggling with this conceptual dilemma to enrich their constellations of theories (Taylor, 1997; Rifkin, Millen, and Cobb, 1991; Feer, 1992). Practitioners must grapple with their own constellations of theories in their own context of dispute resolution when assessing balance and neutrality in any particular mediation session.

Despite any theoretical or context-related differences in views about balance and neutrality, the basic goals are a process that works well enough for each participant, a sense that the mediator is concerned with all of the disputants even while attending to the needs or interests of one, and that all disputants experience the process as supporting their opportunity to participate effectively. When a measure of balance exists, when there is comfort with the interaction, the parties engage in a resourceful and effective manner and the interaction is constructive.

Mediators are managing to achieve balance in the interaction when the disputants experience the mediator as concerned for all of the participants yet impartial and not aligned with any one party; when the mediator is able to maintain an overarching sense of fairness and equity between the parties; and when the parties feel that no disputant is disregarded, left out, or given less attention.

Questions that mediators could ask themselves about the level of balance and neutrality during a session include the following:

- Can each person speak with conviction about important matters without drowning out or overshadowing the other?
- Are the interventions used creating enough movement for both participants?
- Are you providing enough or too much structure? Is the structure inhibiting or restricting anyone's participation?
- When the participants leave, will they still feel good about the interactions when they think of the whole session?

Climate

Everyone has experienced sitting in a staff meeting, a school board session, or a reading group, sensing that the same old issues will be discussed in the same old way, and feeling rather helpless to do anything about it. There is a pervasive sense of collective dread, tight lips, or disengaging frostiness among the people trying to get through this calamitous event. Or imagine participating in a meeting in which discussion is lively and constructive. Participants are unaware of the passage of time and are attentive, active, and engaged in the issues under consideration. Each person has opportunities to contribute, and everyone is focused on a common goal.

Climate refers to the emotional tone in the room, the energy that is being stifled or released, the collective sense of the general tone and context of the interaction as it accumulates. Folger, Poole, and Stutman (1997) present two different definitions of climate. First, "climate represents the prevailing temper, attitudes, and outlook of a dyad, group or organization" (p. 153). This definition describes the attitudes of the participants, the prevailing atmosphere, and the dominant perspective. Second, "climate is the relatively enduring quality of group situation that (1) is experienced in common by group members, and (2) arises from and influences their interaction and behavior" (p. 156). This definition points to the paradox of climate: it is self-created and self-perpetuating yet changeable. Climate both creates the interactions and is created by them. The meeting and balancing of intersecting forces creates the climate, just as in the physical world the forces of gravity, wind, water temperature, and air pressure create an overarching climate that determines the predominant conditions under which things must accommodate themselves and be changed. Yet in the physical world, microclimates are established and can be changed by a shift in the predominant forces—for example, the cutting of the forest canopy, which changes the ground from jungle to desert, and the affects of El Niño and La Niña. In mediation, the participants or the mediator can change the general climate of the session by changing their interactions.

Climates in mediation seem to have four major themes that contribute to the perception of either generativity or ineffectiveness of the group: (1) dominance and authority relations within the system, (2) the degree of supportiveness felt by members of the system, (3) the level of group identity, and (4) the level of autonomy and interdependence in regard to limited resources and competition. These are important factors for mediators to consider when assessing the climate during a particular mediation session or case.

The reciprocal influence of members on the climate and of the climate on members of a system is the key to change. "Critical incidents break up climates either because they make members more aware of themselves or simply because they are so striking that members unconsciously pick up on them and perpetuate new patterns" (Folger, Poole, and Stutman, 1997, p. 171). Mediators serve as the motivators and regulators of this climate during sessions. Courageous acts of change are possible, and such acts can radically alter climates, yet sometimes these bids for change by one member of the system are not sufficient to change the entire climate. Others who do not see an alternative to the present system or who lack the vision to imagine a different situation resist the change.

In mediation sessions, the disputants act out a segment, a microcosm, of their relationship. Although participants in mediation may be able to create a false climate, maintaining a mask of civility that they remove outside the mediation room, there is almost always a moment when the mask slips, if only momentarily, and the true climate, like a blast of cold or hot air, bursts into the mediation.

Although most mediators intend to create positive climates and to reduce negativity and hostility between participants, those who wish to be sensitive to interaction and walk the path of artistry must acknowledge the limits of their ability to manage the interactional climate. The climate will always be determined by the will of the disputants. If one or both have an overarching need to perceive the other as the villain in order to maintain their view of themselves and of the conflict, and if they are determined to hold to that perspective, no effort on the part of the mediator will affect the climate of the interaction. Also, if one person's leitmotif is that "the world tries to do you in," even a pleasant climate in mediation will not be sufficient to bring comfort or a change of perception.

When mediators experience that their efforts at creating a constructive and productive climate during interaction are not sufficient to balance the chill or heat generated by the participants, they should consult their model of mediation for guidance. That model may indicate that they should attempt to clarify the person's feelings or internal conflict, help them voice their concerns about fairness, or otherwise allow the disputants' concerns to emerge. Other models might suggest the use of a caucus to strategize directly with a client. Whatever model or approach, intervention or strategy they choose, mediators must be attentive to each person's internal state. As Folger, Poole, and Stutman (1997, p. 156) note, "People's perceptions play an important role in the creation and maintenance of climate, because these perceptions mediate the effect of climate on people's actions." Focusing only on the general climate in the interaction is insufficient; mediators must also attend to the individual climates of each disputant. Because climate is the barometer reading of interaction, a high or low reading would indicate a need for some additional attention to the individuals and the interaction.

If mediators are conflict avoidant or overcontrolling and afraid to let people express their full range of feelings, the climate can become artificially set at a level of comfort attuned to the mediator and not necessarily to the disputants. In this way, mediators may limit the interaction, never allowing the disputants to surface their deeply felt and potentially contentious points appropriately, because they are frightened of the heat those disagreements create. Similarly, mediators who value a vigorous and intense argument as a means of raising and resolving conflicts may inadvertently increase the heat beyond the comfort level of the disputants. When mediators are secure in their abilities, have a wide range of skills, and are attentive to the changes in the individual and collective climates, they have necessary tools to manage the interactional climate effectively. They can manage anger, they know when clients are moving out of the range of control, and they can facilitate and dissipate the heat through what they do and say. Knowing when a disputant is uncomfortable with the climate is critical to monitoring and adjusting it.

Mediators who are comfortable in a range of climates can also identify overpolite or stiffly correct behavior and encourage disputants to go full throttle in order to help them dig deeper into the conflict. Monitoring and managing the climate will ensure that disputants are not frozen out or that they will not pass out from heat prostration.

The goal for managing the climate of the interactive process is to maintain a safe, hopeful, and open yet organized and flexibly responsive atmosphere in which the conflict is neither too hot to handle nor frozen and unresponsive. In that ideal climate, mediators take active steps to intervene if needed to turn up the heat by focusing attention on the hard issues that allow appropriate conflict to surface, or to turn on the air conditioner to chill down the disputants when they need time to gather their thoughts and emotions.

Reflective questions that mediators might ask themselves about the element of climate in interaction include the following:

- What were the prevailing temper, attitudes, and outlook?
- Did the room ever become too hot or too cool, and what did you or they do?
- Did you allow the disputants to escalate safely until the real issues surfaced?
- Were you able to maintain enough control of the session so that everyone felt safe?
- Did you or they experience the reciprocal effects of the individual and collective climates?
- Is this a room that people would enjoy being in or want to escape from?

Modeling

Professional organizations, including the Academy of Family Mediators, the Association of Family and Conciliation Courts, and the Society for Professionals in Dispute Resolution, assert that one of the highest values in mediation practice is to support client self-determination. If a mediator has truly introjected that concept and is acting consistently with it, his actions and interventions uphold this principle. If mediators are interfering with the disputants' opportunities to reflect on and then adopt certain agreements by leaning on them to make decisions before they are ready, by questioning their capacity to make reasoned and constructive decisions, or by telling them how to deal with their conflicts, those mediators are not acting in accordance with the principle of self-determination. Ultimately, if mediators want the mediation process to have integrity, they must follow this dictum and model the behavior they wish to nurture in the disputants.

Modeling their beliefs requires mediators to walk their talk. If mediators expect good communication, healthy exercise of power, and respectfulness in the session, they must embody these attitudes. If mediators want participants in mediation to be at their best, they must model such behavior. Those mediators who attend to the elements of interaction, managing the process to encourage the broadest range of elements appropriate to the disputants, will provide a sound, effective, ethical, and professional service.

Mediators might use the following questions to assess their level of modeling:

- Are you asking the disputants to do something that you are not doing or are not willing to do?
- Are you acting consistently with your ethics as a person and as a practitioner?
- Are you acting with integrity?

Using Interaction Artistically

The real artistry in interaction is to understand and use these elements to best advantage during mediation sessions. Achieving this level of professional competence requires mediators to assess the elements as they are mediating, to nurture effective communication, and to respond to changes in climate, respectfulness, and other factors as they occur. By focusing on the interaction as it unfolds, mediators call attention to moments when the range of the elements of interaction appear to be constrained or compromised. They note when the application of power is threatening the interaction, when the balance becomes skewed, or when the quality of communication has degraded. In modeling transparency, they present these observations and encourage the disputants to engage in an effort to address the problems. Awareness and assessment of the levels of these interactional qualities is the first step in the process of managing their range. By sharing their observations, mediators bring the disputants into the process of dealing with the problems.

Mediators who are responsive to changes or patterns of interaction are exercising reflection in action. They note the shifts in the interaction and, using reflective methods, explore the possible reasons for the condition. They then experiment, by bringing forward their impressions, observations, and questions and inviting the participants to comment or respond. Mediators hold up a mirror to the participants so they can see for themselves the character of the interaction.

For example, a mediator who is doing this type of reflection in action might state to the participants, when he becomes aware of it, "I get the sense that everyone in the room is walking on eggshells about something, that there is something the two of you are dealing with that you have not shared yet with each other or with me" (a reflection on the element of transparency). In another situation, the mediator might acknowledge the obvious: "Jane, I notice that every time John asks you a question you respond with a negative barb and personal comment against him. Is this the usual pattern of your communication?" (a reflection on their communication, aimed at surfacing a hidden theme of contempt and an invitation to consider whether the comment is patterned behavior). A mediator noticing that the climate in the room is getting more heated and angry might comment, "I sense that there's more heat in the room than there was before, that you are getting to the topics of the conflict that make both of you angry. I wonder how each of you is dealing with that?" (showing awareness of a climate change and asking the participants to confirm or disavow the strength of their emotions and the centrality of the issue).

Mediators must be careful not to offer these impressions too often or in bold or crude ways. To be effective in facilitating the interaction, these comments must be offered with sensitivity to the purpose of making the observation, to the timing of the intervention, and to each participant's readiness to be responsive to the comments. Inviting disputants to participate in this manner requires not only awareness of the interaction by the mediator but also great skill in presenting the opportunity in a way and at a time that helps the participants acknowledge, accept, and use the interaction information to best purpose. Being able to reflect accurately on the elements of interaction with the participants during the course of the mediation process is truly one of the arts of mediation, requiring the attention, sensitivity, and skill of the mediator.

Walking the Path of Artistry

Invite a respected colleague to sit in on a mediation session with you. Ask your colleague to make a list of the topics discussed in this chapter along the left margin of a piece of paper. Then have her draw a line down the middle of the paper and label the left side "positives" and the right side "concerns."

Next ask your colleague to write notes based on the elements of interaction as the session progresses. If possible, it would be helpful for the colleague to write down what was said and who said it, so that you can mentally get back to those moments after the interaction.

Discuss the list with your colleague as soon as the session is over. Try to remain open to your colleagues' impressions and input. Try to find the areas in which you think you need improvement. Go back to your constellation of theories map (see Chapter Five) and note to what extent your actions in the mediation relate to your theories and models.

Looking Back, Looking Forward

The interactive process is the sea in which we swim. When we understand the composition of the sea, we have a new appreciation for its complexity and simplicity. As we understand the elements of the sea, they become more available to us and we have a greater ability to make use of them. As folklore indicates, the sea continues to trap the unwary. If we understand and can predict the tides of interaction, we can better navigate the waters.

Interaction during the mediation session is complex and full of information. It is the field in which we operate, so it is easy to take it for granted and not notice important dimensions. So much occurs during interaction in session that it is critical for mediators to take one step back to understand and assess what is actually going on during the session, while not losing rapport with the disputants or the dynamic quality of being in the session.

We have outlined here the ways in which aware and sensitive mediators might think about and assess the interactions they are having with their clients. The path of artistry requires that mediators interact not just in structured, scripted ways but also in ways that are responsive in the moment to the actual interaction in the room. By becoming more aware of the dimensions of interaction, the reflective mediator can increase artistry. By attending to and responding with subtlety and heightened skill to the swirling forces of relationship, power, communication, and the range of freedom to act, as well as the levels of transparency, respectfulness, and balance and the climate, mediators move gracefully and artistically through the waters of interaction.

In the next chapter we will point out how critical moments during interaction become choice points that require the mediator to use or revise their formulations. They call on mediators to use or change their constellations of theories and require the mediator to act. These critical moments in interaction help us see how all these features work together. Critical moments change interactions and compound to create moments in which artistry resides.

Chapter Eight

Critical Moments in Interaction

Mediators are constantly making choices during the course of a mediation session, and because those choices occur in an instant, mediators are often unaware of their frequency and meaning, and of their consistency with the mediator's constellation of theories and formulation of the case. Just like a car being driven at high speed, a mediator involved in the interaction process is functioning so fast and making minute-by-minute choices that are so complex that it is almost impossible to see all that the mediator is attending to. A critical error in judgment can lead to devastating effects, and small adjustments lead to either staying on course or quickly going off track. Yet these choices accumulate; each moment becomes the building block of the next. Each thing the mediator attends to or lets slide predetermines and sets the stage for the interaction that follows.

Critical moments during interaction in mediation are like the paths diverging in the woods in Robert Frost poem quoted in Chapter Three. They are turning points that, once chosen, set a direction and do not allow a return to that same point to try a different path.

Defining Critical Moments

Critical moments during the interaction and interchange of the mediation session are times when the mediator must fuse the interactive process with reflective practice. The convergence of these two processes creates opportunities that can lead to artistry. Indeed, critical moments demand that the mediator utilize all of the elements of artistic practice that we have been describing. They arise when mediators become aware that they are required by the unfolding events of interaction to make a decision or take some action. What mediators do depends on their formulation, their model or approach, and their theories and core beliefs.

Mediators can know that they are experiencing a critical moment when the interaction demonstrates the following four factors:

- The interaction requires a response from the mediator.
- Multiple responses are available, depending on the mediator's formulation and constellation of theories.
- The mediator senses that it is important to make a decision quickly.
- The moment seems pivotal; that is, the direction, focus, or tone of the mediation will be significantly affected by the mediator's choice of strategy or intervention.

The way the rest of the interaction goes will to some degree be determined by the mediator's response, and then by the subsequent reaction of the participants to that response.

When they experience a critical moment, artistic mediators reflect in action and in the process examine their formulation and assess and use the elements of interactive process. Critical moments offer the mediator specific times and serve as windows of opportunity to assess, confirm, or change their formulations, their theories and models, and the elements of interaction.

Critical moments are opportunities for mediators to reassess their ways of intervening. At such times they feel compelled to select one of three responses: confirm their theories and formulations, change the formulation or the element within their constellation of theories on which it is built, or continue to explore and monitor the interaction, waiting for the next critical moment to happen to see what it will produce. Figure 8.1 places critical moments within the interactional sphere, yet they require reflection in order for the mediator to select one of the three responses.

Critical moments are critical not only to mediators but also to the disputants. If critical moments are handled in unskillful, inartistic, or incomplete ways, the disputants will not get as much value out of the session as they could, and they may even feel that the mediator is not attending to them or is using strategies or practices that do not meet their needs. Critical moments are signals from the disputants that a shift in direction, focus, or approach is needed. If mediators do not see the critical moment and continue oblivious to it, disputants often tune out, become passive, or create power

Figure 8.1. Critical Moments in Interaction.

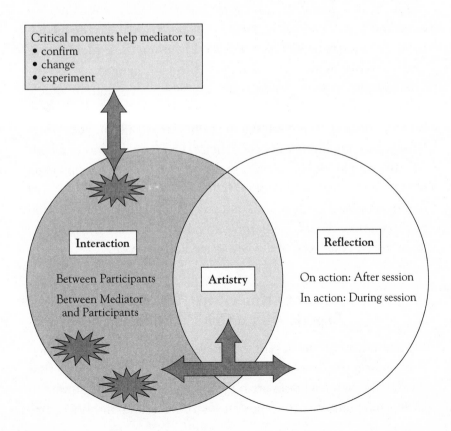

struggles with the mediator, trying desperately to regain the proper course and direction so that the mediation will meet their needs. Critical moments either lead to a sense of trust, rapport, and confidence in the mediator and the interaction, or diminish these factors in the participants' perception.

Critical moments, then, can serve as windows to the mediator's inner world, and they can show the mediator new information about the clients. They become vital links in the mediator's reflective practice. They are part of what mediators need to reflect on after the session is over, and what they must respond to during the session as reflection in action. Unless mediators watch for critical moments during the session, they will see them only after the fact, like hands on a clock that have moved imperceptibly but inexorably to the next numeral on the clock face. When mediators start to use critical moments as tools for reflection, such moments become much more apparent during the session and help the mediator to produce more artistic mediation by using these moments to change one or more of the elements of the interaction.

How mediators respond to critical moments has an indisputable and significant impact on the course and outcome of the mediation. If mediators respond to critical moments artistically and constructively, the cumulative impact of their responses will lead to a constructive and fruitful outcome. Small events, when they accumulate, lead to large-scale differences. Mediations are an accumulation of microevents that compile into outcomes. By paying better attention to those microevents, mediators can positively affect the ultimate meaning and outcome of the whole mediation process.

How to Know That You Are Experiencing a Critical Moment

Mediators know that they are experiencing a critical moment when they feel caught, stuck, or pressured to respond yet are aware that several different responses are possible. Mediators become aware in critical moments that they must make a choice, and the choice they make will depend on their formulation, their constellation of theories, and their sensitivity to the interactive process.

For example, a disputant might ask a mediator, "How do you think we should deal with this problem? What do you think we should do?" Different mediators will respond differently to that particular question, depending on their theories and models. Some mediators will answer the question directly; they value transparency in practice. Some mediators, seeking to gather more information before responding directly, might ask the disputant why they want the mediator to provide the information. Still other mediators might remind the participants that the mediator is an impartial facilitator and not an evaluator, thus using the opportunity to affirm the notion of mediator neutrality. There are numerous other responses, ranging from reflecting back the participant's apparent frustration at not finding a solution, to ignoring the question, to providing a substantive answer. This is a critical moment, in our use of the term, because the choice the mediator makes rests on his or her theoretical orientation and formulation, and it will to some degree determine the rest of the interaction. As we have already noted, mediators who rely on the methods and principles of reflective practice are purposeful and deliberate in their responses to critical moments.

Mediators can often notice critical moments during their interactions when they watch a videotape of their work or when they have the experience at a workshop of stopping a role-play to discuss what just happened. As in forensic science, critical moments can be analyzed after they have occurred. The following scenes from mediation sessions illustrate critical moments and their significance for the interaction.

Examples of Critical Moments in Mediation Sessions

Because critical moments happen in the density of ongoing interaction, examples may help show how the critical moment makes mediators respond, rethink their formulations, or even question their models and theories. The following examples present what critical moments look like in an interaction and how they affect the mediator's formulations and constellation of theories. In workshops we have found that it usually only takes a few moments of interaction before the mediator is faced with a critical moment, and because such moments occur continually, any demonstration or mediation situation is usually rife with them. We have selected a few that show different ways in which such moments and how they are handled can affect the mediation.

Situation 1: Dealing with the Underlying Feelings

(*Note:* We are using a situation we referred to in Chapter Two so that readers can recognize the example but focus on its meaning as a critical moment in interaction.)

Two employees of the same company, Bill and Amy, had been sent as trainers to several company sites. They worked well together and were truly complementary in their skills and approaches to training. One night, as they were celebrating the success of their last training session, Bill had one too many drinks and kissed Amy. When they got back to the home office the next Monday, she filed a sexual harassment grievance. The case was turned over to a mediator, who was working well with them, exploring the past and present of the conflict.

In the dialogue that ensued, the mediator got the sense that the conflict was not about the legalities of the case but about the need for Amy and Bill to reconcile their personal feelings and their professional roles.

> *Amy:* I was offended when Bill kissed me, and really disappointed that this was happening.
>
> *Bill:* Well, I realize that I probably stepped over the line, Amy, but I don't think I deserve to be treated this way, with a grievance filed against me. I didn't harass you!

Mediator: It seems like we are at a choice point here. You both express that you need to deal with the legal issues and with the impact of the situation on your professional relationship, yet I get a sense that the two of you have not yet had a chance to talk in an open way about whatever personal feelings this event has created for you. Would the two of you like to have that opportunity now, before we talk about the other stuff?

Here the mediator sensed a critical moment in which the participants seemed to be dealing with issues other than the legal implications of the grievance. The mediator wondered whether a choice must be made in the focus and direction of the interaction, and he named the critical moment and the issue, leaving to the participants the choice of whether to shift the focus.

This critical moment signaled a change in the mediator's formulation because it changed the way the mediator was thinking about the dispute. It no longer seemed like a dispute over whether legal harassment did or did not happen. Rather, it seemed like a case in which unresolved feelings were interfering with the parties' ability to work together. The mediator, sensing that a change in the formulation might be necessary, invited the disputants to comment on the new formulation.

Situation 2: Contradicting Usual Patterns

In a role-play of a conflict between a supervisor and an employee, which was held in front of observers as a training event for mediators, the female head of a department, Fran, experienced a moment of complete distress when she arrived at work fifteen minutes before an important board meeting to find that her secretary, Barbara, had not typed and photocopied Fran's report. As a result, Fran did not have the materials she needed to support her presentation to the board. Fran was furious, told Barbara her head would roll for this, and stormed out to the board meeting, leaving Barbara shaken and upset. Barbara called the head of human resources (HR), who sent a member of the personnel staff to attempt a crisis mediation with Fran and Barbara.

The mediator tried to convene a joint session, establish ground rules, and specify his role as internal mediator. Fran, who had risen in the company ranks over the previous five years, was not able to listen attentively; her body language conveyed anger, indignation, and a high level of tension. Barbara, with only two years on the job doing word processing and other secretarial functions for the entire department, was still visibly shaken and defensive, alternately sitting quietly then making an emphatically defensive comment.

The mediator believed that separate sessions might help the parties refocus their attention. He met first in a five-minute caucus with Barbara, who asked nervously about losing her job. The mediator talked with Barbara about employee policies regarding hiring and firing. She told Barbara that all employment decisions are made by HR personnel, not by the direct supervisor. Any disciplinary action must be supported by documentation of poor performance, or be based on an immediate threat of harm.

Next, during the individual caucus with Fran, the following dialogue happened:

> *Fran:* I have been here five years and never has anything like this happened to me. I want her out! I want her out today! I am going to walk back into that room and give her this letter. I just won't stand for it. She is going to pay! I am going to get that woman fired! [Fran stood up and headed for the door, with a sealed envelope in hand).
>
> *Mediator:* [Standing and facing Fran from about two feet away] Fran, I know you're upset, and you have not been treated fairly in this situation, but I need you to tell me what's in that letter that you want to give to Barbara.
>
> *Fran:* It's a letter where I tell her she is fired! I am not going to let somebody do this to me and get away with it.

Mediator: [Still standing, close to Fran, blocking her approach to the door of the joint conference room] Fran, it may be that she will end up being fired for this, but I have to tell you that I can't let you take that letter back into mediation. First of all, you know that firing is done by the HR department. Now, I am going to be talking to my supervisor about this situation, and I can tell him your thoughts about this, but I can't let you take that letter into the mediation room. I certainly will bring up your feelings, and Barbara already knows that you want her gone, so we can talk about that in the session. But I need you to calm down a bit and think about what has happened and what you want as an outcome. Why don't you sit down and tell me some more about this.

Fran: [Still standing] What do you mean, sit down! That woman left me to hang it all out in public! I am angry, don't you get it?

Mediator: [Still standing] Yes, I get it, Fran, but I also know that I am not going to let you go in there and further embarrass yourself by handing her a letter that isn't going to be supported by the upper administration. [Fran headed for the door again.] If you go into that room and hand her that letter, I am going to declare the mediation at an end. I can't let you do things that are intimidating in mediation, Fran. Now, it may well be that Barbara will be fired, but that is not your decision. The purpose of mediation is to help figure out what the problems are. So I need your full cooperation to make it work. Now, will you sit back down and go over this with me again? First of all, why don't you tell me how the board meeting went without your report being there? Were you able to tell the board what you needed to tell them?

Fran: [Sitting down on the edge of her seat, slapping the envelope in her other hand] No, not exactly. I mean, I was able to make some sort of an excuse to the board about it and get through the meeting, because I still had my notes, but the full impact of the report was gone. I don't think they are at all pleased, and I don't want this to reflect on my next performance review.

Mediator: [Sitting down] I am sure that we can put a note about this in your file so that if anything comes up about it, you won't take any heat. But tell me why you think this situation got like this?

This was a critical moment for the mediator, because it was obvious that he was going to have to make a choice either to confront the participant or let a level of intimidation happen during the mediation process. If Fran took into joint mediation a piece of paper stating that Barbara was fired, the mediator predicted that both disputants would become reactive again, the mediation effort would break down, and the mediator's credibility with both disputants would be compromised. On the basis of this mediator's constellation of theories and mediation model, the mediator is the guardian of the process, and coercion, intimidation, and overt power plays are not allowable during a session; but a quick spike of reality-based prescriptive information used for confrontation is allowable in extreme situations, so the mediator was acting consistently with his model and theory.

When this situation was explored further with the mediator, another embedded critical moment was revealed: when Fran stood up, the mediator had to make a choice about what to do. Based on the mediator's model, a mediator should always model calmness, and if he had been operating out of that model he would have stayed in the chair, asked the angry and upset disputant to return to her chair, and tried to restate the concerns.

The mediator knew that this split second of the dialogue was a make-or-break moment in which he needed to establish the power to control the mediation session. He needed to make a show of power from a position of strength that could be respected by Fran. The mediator stood and met Fran at eye level until Fran calmed down and returned to her seat. Then the mediator sat down.

On the basis of his theory and practice beliefs, the mediator was actively trying to understand but also divert Fran's anger and feeling of indignance. He was trying to keep her talking until she seemed calmer. The mediator was prepared to allow Fran to ventilate for a few more minutes, then recontract with her about behavior in the joint mediation session. If Fran's emotional temperature had not gone down, or if she had determined not to abide by the rules of mediation, the mediator was prepared to end the mediation session that day and have both disputants take a stress holiday. The mediation effort would have been returned to the head of HR.

This set of critical moments reconfirmed the mediator's formulation of the case regarding the people and the dispute, but it required a change in the third part of the formulation, the method of mediation that would be most effective. It further required the mediator to change an element in his constellation of theories, because the model of mediation he had been taught had not prepared him for the type of situation he confronted. He had learned that the mediator should respect party self-determination, and he did tell the parties how to behave or how to deal with their conflict. Yet the mediator believed that it would have been counterproductive, as well as compromising to his role, to allow Fran to present the letter to Barbara. Although he responded appropriately in the moment, he would need to reflect on action and consider the impact that the events of the mediation would have on the model of mediation he had learned.

In discussions after this role-play experience, the observers were able to question the person playing the role of Fran about whether this active, stand-up confrontation had truly been helpful, because this action did not fit into their models of mediation and their constellations of theories. The woman who played Fran acknowledged that she would have had no respect for the mediator at all or for the mediation process itself if the mediator had continued to sit in the chair and talked calmly. She confirmed that in her role as Fran, she needed the mediator to confront her actively to show her who had the power and to show that the mediator was not intimidated by her. When the mediator stood up and continued standing eye to eye with Fran, Fran was then able to trust and respect the mediator as having enough personal power to be helpful to the situation. She was then willing to cooperate with the rest of the process.

For many of the observers, this was a confusing and frustrating moment, because the mediator's intervention seemed necessary and appropriate yet was directly contradictory to their model. The observers had to find a way of making sense out of this discrepancy. For some observers, this role-play was a call to review their model to decide whether confrontation is ever necessary or appropriate. For others, it was too jarring, and they refused to see that their paradigms needed to change, that they could not hold onto the model they had learned and also value the approach taken by the mediator. So they argued with the role-players, insisting that confrontation with a client could never be good. The woman playing Fran continued to state steadfastly that this had been the right intervention, that the standing and confrontation contributed to rather than diminished the genuineness, trustworthiness, and credibility of the mediator and the mediation process for that participant.

Situation 3: Roles and Power Struggles

In this conflict situation, an apprentice mediator was co-mediating with a more experienced family mediator in order to receive feedback and support during his initial six cases, a process required by the state in which he resided in order to qualify for court-connected domestic-relation case referrals. The case involved nonmarried parents whose one mutual child, eight years old, was spending every other weekend with the father and who had always resided primarily with the mother. The father had brought a pro se case before the court, requesting change of custody, but what he really wanted was expanded parenting time—half of the summer and all of the holidays. The mother had been thinking of curtailing the current visitation plan because she was concerned about lax supervision, as well as about her daughter's exposure to drinking and smoking during visits with her father. The father was a self-recovered alcoholic; the mother was a self-confessed born-again Christian who had foresworn all alcohol and had married a man of similar beliefs.

The climate of the room grew more and more tense and the level of disregard and lack of respectfulness the mother had for the father was obvious in her interactions. The apprentice mediator was struggling to deal with the father's constant defensive attacks toward the mediator. The supervising co-mediator decided to wait until the next critical moment to intervene, in order to help the apprentice mediator experience and reformulate for himself how to deal effectively with the interaction.

> *Apprentice mediator:* [to the father] So, you are saying that you want more time with your daughter, but when mom here asks you to control your environment, by stating to your friends that they can't smoke or drink when your daughter is with you, you say you can't impose that rule on them.
>
> *Father:* That's right. What they do is their own business. I am not going to tell them not to drink a beer if they come over.
>
> *Mother:* No, and that's the problem. You've told them they can't come in because she's with you, and she feels guilty about that. That's part of why she doesn't want to come over any more.
>
> *Father:* Well, I still want half the summer. You told me that if I quit drinking, I could have her more, and I did. And then it's always something else, some other excuse to keep me from having her. I did what you asked, and now I'm going to make sure I get her half the time because I deserve it. Fair's fair. I live for my daughter. I think you are way overprotective. A kid's gotta be a kid, roam around in the woods a little, just be free, not sitting in the house like you make her do. When she's with me she gets to play with other kids, like a kid ought to.

The mother looking away and down, turning her body away from the father, obviously shutting down and stonewalling.

> *Apprentice mediator:* [Obviously frustrated with the father and feeling out of control] Well, Dad, what do you think is the basis of asking for more time other than the fact that you want it? How is more time with you in the child's best interest?
>
> *Father:* She needs to be more free, I tell you. That's what I have to offer her, her childhood. That's why she needs to be with me at least half the summer.
>
> *Mother:* But she doesn't want to be with you! She thinks your place is filthy, and she's allergic to smoke!
>
> *Father:* But I don't smoke around her. I go outside to smoke whenever she's with me. And I can't help it if she gets a little whiff if she's outside.

This is a case of lost critical moments in the interaction. There were several critical moments that the mediator could have used effectively but, due to his inexperience, he did not, and the co-mediator did not respond because of the requirement to let the mediator learn by doing. When the mediator experienced the tension and power struggle between himself and the father, he could have named it as such and invited the father to respond to this observation. The mediator might also have taken a moment to reflect on the father's behavior, and perhaps would have developed a formulation that would have taken into account how the mediator's critical comments to the father may have provoked the power struggle. Other critical moments became apparent, including when the mother physically and emotionally turned away and when she snapped back at the father. The mediator could have used either critical moment to help the participants acknowledge and then deal with the substantive issues in their dispute. The mediator might also have taken the opportunity to develop a formulation to explain the hostility and bitterness. He also did not see another critical moment, the flash of anger by the father. There was an unspoken message in this moment, from dad to mom: "You don't trust me and you are trying to control me, and I won't put up with it." Equally, there was an unspoken message from mom to dad: "I'm the custodial parent, I have all the power here, and I can disregard you, because you can't afford to take me to court, and you'll lose if you try. I don't have to give you anything."

The mediator did not seize the moments for best use. His formulation about the case was incomplete and unhelpful. He judged the father as a hopeless "dry drunk," who was more interested in parity with the mother than in the quality of his relationship with his daughter. In so characterizing the father, the mediator was unaware that his own judgments about the father were potentially interfering with the mediator's ability to be responsive and helpful to the parties.

The apprentice mediator did not appear to operate from a particular model, nor did he indicate awareness of a constellation of theories that was supporting his interaction with the participants. He did not see how his own behavior and words had altered the interaction. In sum, he did not recognize or see the value of the critical moments that occurred during the interaction.

Noticing Critical Moments in Action

Critical moments are often like Russian wooden nesting dolls—moments inside moments inside moments. Mediators sense them, but often do not take the time to analyze them. Reflective practice relies on a mediator finding and utilizing these critical moments, reflecting on them after they have happened, and even becoming more aware of them during the session, while they are happening.

The first question to ask yourself in order to identify a critical moment is, *Do I know a critical moment when it appears?* Some of the hallmarks of critical moments are that mediators start to feel their own reactions to interactions; they feel impelled to initiate or stop an intervention, to take some action. On a physical level, mediators often experience their face flush, their body get tense, their anger rise. They can hear an inner voice saying that there is danger, that the situation is at risk of getting out of control, or that there is a remarkable opportunity to influence the course of the interaction and something needs to be done immediately. If mediators have concerns about their own competencies and knowledge, they may even register the critical moment as an internal, critical voice that is saying the equivalent of, "Oh, oh! Now you've blown it!" The mediator's internal monitor is subliminally registering the changes in the interaction, even if the mediator is not attentive or fully aware.

The more mediators are aware of their own reactions, the more they might register that they and the disputants are experiencing a critical moment. If the mediator is aware of the critical moment, it is highly likely that the disputants are also sensing that they are at a fork in the road. If mediators are creatively attending to their own reactions, using themselves as the barometer of the elements in the interaction, they will know when the time for action and choice has arrived.

Another question to ask in order to learn how to make effective use of critical moments is, *What is my usual pattern when I sense a critical moment?* Some mediators grow quiet, frightened to do anything for fear that they will make the wrong decision. Others continue their interventions according to their models, in effect denying that a critical moment is happening. Still others use that moment to share their sense of heightened awareness with the disputants, as part of the transparency they maintain between their experience and the disputants. Mediators' responses to critical moments are often patterned and unconscious responses that show how they feel about themselves and their role. Mediators who feel insecure about their competency might well follow a patterned response of covering over the moment, not noticing it, or shying away from it. Mediators who embrace the methods and principles of reflective practice, however, eagerly await critical moments, seeing them as opportunities to broaden their understanding of their constellation of theories, to assess their formulations, and in general to learn from the experience.

When mediators notice a critical moment during an interaction, the first step is to acknowledge to themselves that they are at a choice point. Before sharing their impressions with the disputants, they reflect in action, attempting to make some sense out of the critical moment. They then offer their observations to the disputants. Announcing that a critical moment exists is like announcing that you are experiencing a moment of déjà vu—it alters the experience enough so that it can be coped with differently. After making known the critical moment and their observations, mediators who practice from principles that require active choice by the disputants might then want to offer the disputants the three choices (continue, change, or experiment) rather than make the choice themselves. These three choices can be elaborated to the disputants so they can fully understand their options.

For example, a mediator who notices that she is getting angry at a disputant who is balking at continuing to negotiate might want to use that internal signal to verify that a critical moment is happening. Using the method of reflection in action, the mediator might ask herself why this disputant is balking and why his behavior has provoked an angry response from her. Using the information in the interaction and her constellation of theories, the mediator might uncover a formulation that explains the pattern she has observed—possibly that she had been inattentive to the disputant's growing frustration, which is now manifesting as balking at negotiation. Having developed a formulation, the mediator could then state to the client, "I am aware that I am feeling frustrated, and I think it has something to do with the slowness of the negotiation between the two of you. Are either of you having similar feelings, and do either of you want to do something different to help this situation?" By acknowledging the internal signal (I feel something, I need to do something), then reflecting in action and finally acknowledging the critical moment to the disputants (you have to make a choice), the mediator allows it to surface into the interaction and tries to engage the disputants in dealing with it.

Taking Risks

Critical moments are occasions to consider taking risks. Mediators who practice artistically see in critical moments the potential of the mediation process. They appreciate the possibilities; they are visionary. To maximize the value of critical moments, mediators may need to take risks. They should take these risks wisely and deliberately and only after considering the benefits and the liabilities. Using critical moments as opportunities to reflect in action, to assess the validity and relevance of their formulation and their constellation of theories, and to examine the elements of the interaction, mediators reevaluate whether their operating assumptions are correct or whether another valid approach might be more useful. Like hikers on a journey into unfamiliar terrain, who rely on maps, equipment, physical condition, and experience to guide them safely, mediators use their knowledge and skills, together with reflective practice and interactive process, to explore the terrain of the mediation.

Critical moments require responsiveness on the part of the mediator. Sometimes the most constructive and fitting responses make mediators feel as if they are out on a limb. They sometimes feel pulled along by the disputants, as if the disputants are showing the mediator, by their interaction, that something needs to be done, that they have shifted gears or altered direction and the mediator needs to join them. The three most common aspects that need to change at critical moments are the mediator's formulation, the theoretical concepts the mediator brings to the critical moment from his or her constellation of theories, and the elements of interaction. If mediators can respond appropriately and know which aspect to change, they can bring about greater artistry. The element that needs to change is revealed through the use of the methods of reflection in action and reflection on action.

At critical moments, mediators may choose to mark the moment, to acknowledge that they perceive a difference in the interaction but have elected to wait and see what will occur next. Simply acknowledging the existence of a critical moment changes the moment; the mediator has become aware of the choice point and has made explicit that which had been implicit. Noticing and acknowledging the moment provides an opportunity for mediators to make conscious, purposeful choices about subsequent strategies and interventions.

Naming a phenomenon often changes its dynamic; no longer nameless and formless, a shadow, it is now a bright light. One choice for mediators who have noticed the critical moment is to observe and take no further steps to alter the interaction, their formulation, or their theories. Suspending the need to do more than mark the moment can be difficult. Silence can be as risky as any other intervention. Mediators are taught to act, to engage. Observing without action seems passive, as though the mediator was withdrawing from the interaction. To the contrary, allowing the interaction to unfold represents a deliberate choice to gather more information. The mediator may sense that the disputants are not yet ready to address a new issue, or for other reasons the time is not ripe for a more active intervention.

To experiment in response to critical moments may leave mediators and disputants with some sense of ambiguity about the direction the mediation may then take. The process of exploration leads to discovery of something new. The tools needed for exploration are the elements of a beginner's mind: curiosity and a willingness to move ahead without judging, classifying, or requiring certainty. This approach requires a different way of knowing. Often critical moments may not resonate with what the mediator knows or has experienced before. Critical moments are new, fresh, and nascent with possibility. They are gifts waiting to be opened.

Critical moments are all around us, if we are open to them. In role-play experiences and in seminars and conferences, we have found that it takes only two to three minutes to reach a critical moment. And as the Frost poem reminds us, taking one road necessarily excludes exploration of the other. Mediations are constructed of moments, each of which may seem unimportant, but taken together they constitute the whole, the gestalt of the mediation.

Walking the Path of Artistry

We invite you to use critical moments in your next mediation as opportunities to discover these wonderful unopened gifts of experience. The next few times you mediate, remember to remain aware of what your body and mind are telling you. If you experience a critical moment, when you know a choice needs to be made, take advantage of the moment by using the methods of reflection in action. Slow the process, investigate the source of your awareness, take the following steps. Once you have reflected on the circumstances of the critical moment, you may want to share your impressions with the disputants and make them colleagues in determining what needs to change. To move from awareness of the critical moment to a decision to intervene, proceed along the following path:

- Acknowledge the perception that you are at a crossroads, a turning point, a critical moment.
- Describe why you think the interaction is a critical moment—what you are aware is different, what has become a pattern in interaction, or what you are feeling.
- Using the process of reflection in action, consider whether your formulation is constructive and fits the disputants and their conflict. Explore your constellation of theories to determine whether there are elements that will help explain the phenomenon of this critical moment.
- Create an experiment to test the validity and suitability of your formulation. One possible experiment is to ask for feed-

back from the disputants—Are they experiencing the critical moment? You might ask whether they also feel that things are stuck, that something is not working, or that there are ripe opportunities to move the process forward.

- Collaborate in determining the next step. Share with the disputants what would be your tendency or inclination at this point, and see whether they agree or disagree with that direction. If they disagree, put them in charge of finding the next step, and wait to see where and how they will take the interaction.

To follow this procedure, you have to be willing to believe that the participants in mediation are able to discover and do what they need. It is a method that firmly rests on transparency of process and a belief that you can trust the disputants to find their own solutions with your active involvement. The process thus requires a firm belief that the clients have the capacity and the willingness to be self-determining.

You may discover that the clients eagerly and actively take up the invitation to engage in thinking about and responding to the critical moments. They may firmly grasp the opportunity of self-determination. Such a positive response would confirm that the model being used suits the disputants or that the formulation was accurate and useful. Conversely, the clients may be unwilling or unable to accept the opportunity to participate in the decisions that shape the interaction. If they decline the invitation to collaborate, it may signal a need to reassess the model of mediation employed, to question its suitability for these disputants, or to question the formulation that suggested that the disputants would be interested in a collaborative approach.

The process of questioning formulations and models leads to an understanding of why certain approaches work well or poorly. These discoveries lead to a heightened level of competence and increased effectiveness. You are learning not simply what interventions are effective or unresponsive, but also what causes them to fit some situations and be unsuitable in others. This process of exploration and discovery leads to greater self-awareness, and ultimately to artistry.

Looking Back, Looking Forward

Critical moments are embedded in the constantly accumulating interactions of the mediation. They are choice points, opportunities for discovery, insight, and change. Mediators' choices will be based on their constellations of theories, their formulations of cases, and their assessment of the range of the elements of interactions.

If mediators are acting as reflective practitioners, they may be able to gain insights from these critical moments and use them to change one or more elements of the interaction between the disputants. Because heightened awareness and sensitivity are signs of true artistry, the more mediators are aware of and respond to these critical moments and the more they utilize them during interaction, the more they will bring artistry to the process. When mediators make effective use of critical moments, their cumulative responses result in a constructive and positive process and outcome.

Having looked at the elements of interaction that can lead to artistry and then at the critical moments in interaction that hold the possibility for artistry, we will now focus on another way of understanding artistry in interaction—the experience of flow. When the elements of interaction (relationship, power, communication, modeling) are working artistically and when critical moments are handled with skill and sensitivity, the outcome of this artistry in interaction is the unique experience of flow for the participants and the mediator.

Chapter Nine

Finding and Keeping the Flow

The words of Lao Tsu from the 6th century B.C. in China, which are quoted in the front of the book, are testimony to the concept that flow has been around as long as humankind has been conscious: Flow has been described at various times as that sense of deep concentration, absorption, joy, and accomplishment that are some of the best benefits of being human. As a feeling that merges thought and body, flow becomes the payoff for hard but artistically done work, the product that everyone desires.

The hallmarks of artistry described in Chapter Two identify the particular behaviors, language, and attitudes that characterize an artistic performance. They depict the observable actions that distinguish artistic approach. Flow is the uniquely personal experience of artistry in practice. Although other people can attribute certain behaviors they may observe to artistry, only the person who is experiencing flow can sense and understand that experience. In mediation, flow is the experience of working artistically, through the processes of heightened interaction and reflection. It is felt by the participants and the mediator when artistry exists.

Flow as an experience is built into everyone's physiology as well as into everyone's mental state. Everyone has the capacity to feel flow. To achieve this state, however, requires a level of skill, knowledge, and discipline; thus it is available only to those who are ready for artistry in their endeavors, whether mountain climbing, dancing, or mediating. It could almost be said that flow is both the process and the product of artistry.

Defining Flow

People experiencing the state of flow have a goal they are trying to achieve, and they receive feedback along in the process that indicates very close approximation to the ideal. They are using their well-honed skills in order to arrive at this level of ideal approximation, and their skills match the requirements. When in this state, their conscious awareness and their abilities seem unitary and simultaneous. During the state, everything irrelevant and interruptive drops away, and ordinary thoughts or worries vanish. People feel powerful when in this state, totally focused on the present, so as to have a dual sense of being both unselfconscious and at the same time totally aware and submerged in the experience. It is paradoxical. They feel the lack of self and the fullness of self. They often report feeling caught up in something greater than usual, a transcendence of purpose and process. Perhaps the most telling feature is the experience of time distortions—the moment seems both longer and shorter, or there is no sense of time at all. For all these reasons, the experience of flow is a powerful, rewarding one, which becomes self-perpetuating because of its own intrinsic rewards. People tend to seek opportunities to experience flow, to have these peak moments, because they exhilarate without exhausting.

Mihaly Csikszentmihalyi (1991, 1993, 1996, 1997) has studied the experience and process of flow by using physiological psychology methods and tests, and by collecting personal statements from diverse people. His synthesis of these data has indicated that there are eight characteristic dimensions of the experience of flow. These can be applied to mediation practice as follows:

1. Artistry in mediation practice begins with a clear sense of purpose, an understanding of the mediator's role in the process. Mediators must understand the theories, principles, beliefs, and values that shape their actions. Among those principles are notions about the goals of mediation and the appropriate role for the medi-

ator. Awareness of these matters is essential to the experience of flow and artistry.

Having appropriate and readily accessible feedback loops is vital to artistic practice and to the experience of flow. Reflective supervision and peer consultation nurture the mediator's exploration of the terrain of mediation practice. In addition, engaging disputants or co-mediators in reflecting on the critical moments of an interaction provides a rich source of information about the development of formulations, the appropriateness of models, and the usefulness of interventions.

2. A precondition to artistry in practice is having knowledge (a constellation of theories) and proficiency in using an array of practice skills. Earlier chapters presented the notion that mediators cannot attain artistry unless they have a level of competency in both knowledge and skills. They need adequate verbal skills and interviewing techniques, an understanding of the principles of mediation and negotiation, and a repertoire of techniques and skills. Moreover, these skills and knowledge must be appropriate for the types of disputes they mediate, and they must have the experience of being resourceful in the application of their knowledge and skills.

3. Mediators experience flow in their practices when their concentration is so heightened and the interaction is so compelling that their interventions take on a fluid, seemingly unconscious or intuitive quality. They experience a heightened sensitivity to the subtle interactional cues that signal critical moments. Mediators in flow also experience an effortlessness in designing and implementing interventions, a sense of doing without forcing.

4. Mediators whose level of concentration is such that they are oblivious to the events outside the interaction focus on the disputants and their interaction, attending to the moment-to-moment shifts, the patterns of behavior, and the language, as well as to the content. They are experiencing that ultimate concentration of flow and artistry.

5. By virtue of their positions and the trust placed in them by the disputants, mediators are in a position to use their skills to help parties achieve their objectives. The potential for manipulation, for carrying out the mediator's goals rather than the goals of the parties, is always present. Consistent use of feedback loops, engaging the disputants in the management of the interaction, and adhering to the principles of reflective practice will help guard against the pernicious use of the mediator's power.

6. When mediators experience flow, it is as if they have discovered what they knew all along. The urge to improve their practice urges mediators intrinsically to higher levels of complexity, and therefore to higher and higher levels of gratification. Mediators and others are not addicted to flow; they are not helpless compulsives who cannot stop, like the dancer in Hans Christian Andersen's story *The Red Shoes,* who must continue dancing until death overtakes her. Flow is more like being at the apex of the mediator's skill, so it is a highly desirable if ephemeral state.

7. When mediators are aware of and attentive to the interactions in a session and fully engrossed in reflection during a mediation, they experience full connection with the disputants and the interaction of the mediation process. They are so absorbed in the quality, focus, and intent of the interaction that they experience an altered sense of time. Every moment both lengthens and shortens, and the mediation session goes by in an instant.

8. Flow is not just a pleasant feeling the mediator is trying to have. It has actual benefits that are measurable: increased productivity, heightened self-esteem, and enhanced creativity. The lack of flow experiences leads to disappointment, a sense of lost opportunities and failed interventions, of flatness or ennui. By contrast, the experience of artistry in practice is exhilarating, stimulating, and inspiring.

If any of these signs is present, the mediator is experiencing some level of flow. When in flow, mediators are oblivious of outside distractions and aware of every aspect of the interaction; they are less calculating and more open to what is actually going on. The goal of this chapter is to help mediators become more aware of the value of flow and then to increase the opportunities to experience it in their practice.

Mediators are not the only participants to experience flow in the interactional process. The disputants are part of the interaction and will also sense when the process and results have the qualities of flow. There are times in artistic mediation when both the participants and the mediator are so fully engrossed in the interchanges, so fully engaged in the mental and emotional content, and so sensitive to the interaction among them that the experience flows for each of them. During flow, all the elements of interaction, defined in Chapter Seven, are functioning in the broadest possible range and to such a degree that the interaction feels right and inspiring, and the mediator feels wise and discerning.

At their best moments in mediation, most mediators are experiencing a flow state, and the experience is so engaging and fulfilling that they want to achieve flow more often in their practices. Think back to some of your most successful cases, where there was not only a favorable outcome but also a sense that the means were as important as the outcome. When such experiences are measured against the criteria of flow, we predict that at least sometimes you and your clients experienced flow. It is because of their experience of the mediator's artistry that even participants who do not reach actual agreements in their mediation express satisfaction with the mediation process. Flow feels good, for the mediator and the disputants.

The experience of flow is not subject to the will of the mediator. It is the product of right relationship in interaction and the appropriate use of formulations and the constellation of theories. Although mediators cannot demand or command flow, they can promote the conditions that lead to the experience of flow. As we have said, having the experience of flow is a signal to mediators that they are on the path toward artistry. At such times the mediator's level of technical expertise emerges in such skillful ways that it frees the mediator to seek the nuances in interaction and to use critical moments to best advantage. It also means that the mediator is using all of his or her powers of reflection to modulate the interactions.

All people have had random moments of flow in one or more arenas of their lives and in all sorts of activities and endeavors: from making music to making love, from rock climbing to sewing, from relating to children in a classroom to the solitary effort of gardening. When we were writing this book, both of us at times were so engrossed in writing, so engaged in trying to bring the inner experience of mediation into words, that we lost track of time. Both of us had times when we were in flow, oblivious to the hour, the sounds in the next room, the weather outside, the dog, and everything except the process of giving voice to our ideas and experiences. We were so fully involved that we were unaware of our surroundings yet felt ourselves to be fully aware of what we were thinking about and entering into the computer. It is this experience of being most fully oneself, and being beyond oneself, that is characteristic of the inner experience of being in flow, and what makes it, like other peak experiences in life, something to be pursued. We focus on this personal experience of flow because it is an indicator of artistry.

Flow is ultimately practical. It is not just a feel-good experience for the person who is in it. It produces practical results; it is creative and productive. For this reason, it makes good, hard business sense to try to be in flow more often in mediation. The clients like the experience and get better results, and the mediator likes the experience and gets less burnout and angst. Flow is available and useful to all.

A recent article by Piercy and Nelson (1999) indicates that social workers and therapists, who like mediators work in an interactive process, are also aware of experiencing this sense of flow during and after the sessions they consider to be successful. Like mediators, counselors and therapists cannot make decisions for their clients, and they must maintain a balance of appropriate professional distance and a quality of relationship and genuineness that engenders trust in order to work successfully in the interactions they have with their clients. Like mediators, they need to be reflective and responsive, because their interactive process also accumulates moment by moment. Because mediators share so many features of interactive process with counselors and therapists, it is heartening to note that they also describe this experience of flow, of being fully oneself yet transcendent, and its results as the epitome of excellence and artistry. Piercy and Nelson describe the foundation for achieving flow in practice as follows: "The fundamental prerequisite for flow experiences in therapy is having so much confidence in the process and in your abilities that you can focus in the present and know you don't have to control everything or say just the right thing or make someone else's pain go away. Too much effort to 'do' therapy cuts you off from your best resource—yourself" (p. 46).

These conditions also apply to the interactive process of mediation. Mediators are their own best resource, and allowing flow to happen enables a heightened sense of self-esteem to emerge into the unself-conscious responsiveness we have been describing as artistic mediation practice.

Signs of Flow

Knowing the signs of flow can help mediators recognize whether they have experienced it in their mediation sessions. To assess whether you are having a flow experience, you could ask yourself the following questions during or after the session as part of your reflective practice. Try to analyze the elements of the interaction, however, using the list of factors provided in Chapter Seven, to learn which features were predominant when flow existed.

- Do you have the type of connection to disputants that provides the opportunity for the feedback needed to support flow?
- Are your skills and experience well suited to the dispute and to managing the interaction for the disputants?

- Do you lose track of time in the mediation session, to the point that you almost forget to end on time?

- When you end the session, does it feel as though you have been in session only a half an hour when according to the clock it has been much longer?

- Have you ever had a mediation that lasted a long time and you actually felt better when you came out than when you went in?

- Are you able to appreciate the possibilities embedded in the mediation?

If flow is happening, your answers to these questions should be yes, at least sometimes. Flow is not a constant state but comes and goes in the interaction. Because the mediator is not solely responsible for making flow happen, do not feel too distressed if these signs are not present for an entire session or in each case. Like the path to artistry, flow is a journey, not a destination. Aspire to the experience of flow in practice, apply the methods and principles of reflective practice and interactional process, and then note when flow occurs.

An example that illustrates the signs of flow may help make this hard-to-describe experience more understandable. When a couple came to mediation, they had already experienced nine years of difficult and heated divorce-related conflict, both in obtaining the divorce and for the eight years subsequently. The current dilemma for which they were seeking mediation was the resolution of three specific issues: unpaid marital settlement debts, the value of a video camera that had been transferred, and the division of family pictures that also had not been transferred from one party to the other as required under the original divorce decree.

The father was a highly competitive businessman whose failure in business had been a contributing factor in the breakdown of the marriage. The mother was a frail beauty, whose presentation of self belied her strength to wage war with her former husband all this time, and to resist his efforts to renegotiate issues that had once been settled. She was demanding that he perform on his stated agreements and was no longer giving him room to negotiate. They both were very much aware, each having been in therapy, of the role each played in this continuing drama. However, when they appeared for mediation, they insisted that all they needed and wanted to talk about was a strict problem-solving approach to resolving the final items of business.

The mediator sensed that the presenting problem (what to do about the camera, photos, and past-due payments) was the tip of the iceberg, and that a strong need for negative intimacy and revenge, along with unexpressed power dynamics, was operating. When the mediator reflected this formulation to them, the clients held firm to their request for a problem-solving process that would lead to a written agreement about the camera, the pictures, and the payments. The mediator might have developed an initial formulation based on a perceived ethical dilemma, with contradictory demands of "let the clients decide" versus "be fair." The interaction between the clients suggested two possible additional formulations of the people and the problem: either that this was simple revenge or that the people were showing undiagnosed or untreated personal pathology. The mediator sensed that the continuing conflict might be connected to an ungrieved loss, a story neither of the parties had ever been allowed to tell to the right person, masked as it was by such bitter animosity and angry behaviors. They had been allowed to tell it to their therapists and to the children, but they had not had an opportunity and the setting in which to share their stories with each other.

The mediator sensed the personal readiness of the disputants to lay down this very heavy sword of recrimination and bitterness and end the battle. It appeared that both parties wanted the hostility to stop, yet each was unwilling to be perceived by the other as the loser. These impressions came to the mediator through the combination of all the clients' gestures, body language, tone of voice, and word choices, as well as the history of the conflict as presented by each party during the interaction. Because the mediator was able to get to a place of flow, these impressions were not discounted or dismissed but rather were part of an intricate and fine web that was being created in the interaction. On the basis of these impressions, and relying on her evolving formulation of ungrieved losses never allowed to surface rather than personal pathology, the mediator decided to engage in an experiment with the clients to learn whether the formulation was accurate and useful.

The mediator contracted with the clients that she would start with the stated problem-solving agenda (this is, just a conflict about the camera, pictures, and payment) until they experienced that the old pattern of interacting was reappearing, and then the mediator would try a different tactic with them. The clients agreed, partly because they appreciated the transparent process and partly because they knew they would run up against the same old barriers that kept them from reaching agreement. Within five minutes of keeping to the stated agenda, the woman wandered off into a diatribe about the past, and the man bargained and cajoled her as usual. The dysfunctional pattern of interaction that impaired their ability to resolve the conflict had resurfaced.

Because the mediator had set the stage for the possible occurrence and because she was able to maintain the sense of flow, the critical moment became apparent to everyone in the room. Silence came over them. The mediator calmly stated that the moment had come to try something different.

The mediator then noted that the tone in the room was of pain and loss, not the usual anger. In almost a whisper, she asked the couple to talk to each other, from their hearts, about what they had lost through the divorce. Each one told a poignant tale, the former wife declaring that the husband had "ruined the family and scarred the boys for life," in ways that she could see every day. Because it was now being said in a less angry and hostile, blaming way, her former husband could hear her story. He also told a tale of loss of family life and the ideal he had held for their marriage. He then acknowledged how he had actively tried to manipulate her with money. She responded, telling him how she had actively tried to get back at him through her resistance and coldness. At one point they were near tears. They turned to each other, asked forgiveness, and truly and deeply apologized for the hurt they had caused each other and their children. It was a moment that sent chills down the mediator's spine, due to the sincerity and heartfeltness of the moment. The flow was apparent in the participants' responses. What had been so difficult for so many years now seemed to flow so easily for them. It was a powerful moment for everyone in the room.

Then the moment passed, and the mediator picked up the thread of interaction by reminding the participants of their need to stop using disagreements over cameras, pictures, and unpaid debts to get back at one another for the losses they had suffered through the divorce. The focus of attention shifted effortlessly back to the specific topics they had come to discuss. It was a moment of flow for all, for it would not have happened had the mediator not taken the risk of stepping out of the stated aim of the session. The mediator noticed the parties' behavior, language, and tone and developed a formulation that ultimately led to the experiment that in turn produced the experience of flow. Having acknowledged their loss and pain, the couple were able to go back to solving the problems that had brought them to mediation. They left with an agreement about the pictures, the payment, and the camera, but also with a sense that they could lay down the struggle because the meaning had really finally been expressed.

What brought each of them to the ability to respond in that moment in the way they did? We would like to think of it as the creativity inherent in the process of mediation. The hallmarks of flow were there—openness, feeling beyond time, being caught up in the rapids of interaction, and the passion and compassion. The high level of skill and artistry the mediator brought to the situation served as the springboard for the intervention that contributed to flow. The mediator left the session feeling honored to have been a participant in such a transformative experience. The parents walked out having experienced a new reality. This was flow, and traveling the path to artistry.

Blocks to Flow

We would not expect novice mediators to find flow frequently, because they do not have the requisite level of knowledge and skill or the mediation experience to achieve artistic interactions. Apprentices likely have enough flow experiences to make them hunger for more. If mediators are not finding flow to be a consistent or frequent experience after they have advanced from novice or apprentice to practitioner, they might want to reflect on their mediations and determine whether there is something blocking them from experiencing this state.

There are many possible explanations for the lack of flow in practice. Is the mediator afraid that his or her skills are not up to the challenges being presented by the disputants? Mediators can experience flow only if there is a fit between their skills and knowledge base and the demands of the particular dispute or the unique needs of the disputants. If the situations are truly out of their league, then mediators cannot experience flow, because they cannot respond functionally, let alone artistically.

Lack of flow often happens when administrative or judicial systems force mediators to take cases that are far too complex or emotionally dynamic or not ripe. To achieve artistry in their practices, novices and apprentices need support, guidance, and supervision. Administrators need to support co-mediation and peer review processes that help present and demonstrate artistic mediation practice.

Lack of flow might also be an indicator of a need to go back for additional training or supervision in order to deal with certain kinds of cases, or it might indicate a need to create more effective formulations, broaden a conceptual foundation in the constellation of theories, or become more aware of the critical moments in interaction. A very constructive approach for such situations would be to have a more experienced mediator, acting as a mentor, sit in on mediation sessions. Mediators with a limited foundation in theory might read more extensively to build up their constellation of theory. Mediators might also use the exercises in this book and review their mediation sessions in terms of the interactional process.

If flow is blocked by the fear of losing control when in the flow state, mediators might want to ask themselves, What was the worst thing I ever did when I lost control? If the mediator experienced some genuine trauma or serious negative consequence that affects his or her ability to mediate, then there is good reason for resistance to experiencing flow. A mediator may also hold a belief that good mediators "don't do flow." Those who hold the strong ethical value "First, do no harm" can be trying to ensure that no harm will occur by blocking themselves from having the fullness of the flow experience.

Perhaps a mediator has discovered that the block to experiencing flow is that he or she is easily distracted, confused, or unable to concentrate fully. The distraction may be physical pain or emotional distress, or it may be background noises, such as jangling phones and whirring fax machines, or constant interruptions. Many mediators work at the disputants' site rather than at their own office and must accommodate uncomfortable, inadequate, or noisy surroundings.

If mediators are unable to lose a sense of time, an essential of the experience of flow, it may be because they practice mediation in a system that imposes an industrial, production-line model on the mediation's interactional process. If the mediator and the disputants are in flow, can they take that extra fifteen minutes or half hour to finish and come to a real closure spot, or must the mediator end the session because time on the parking meters is running out or the agency is closing or the next clients are waiting? Those who mediate in public sector positions and seek flow in their practices must ensure that the mediation process is not co-opted by the demands of the larger system for caseload management and outcome accountability. To experience flow, mediators must ensure that they have the necessary and sufficient personal, social, and structural conditions.

A mediation intern completing a routine part of fact gathering suddenly sensed, from something one of the disputants said, that the client had a gun in her purse. It was apparent to the other co-mediator that something had happened, because the intern was not listening attentively and seemed distracted. When there was a break in the conversation, the intern rushed in with a comment that diverted the client's attention in an unproductive direction, wasting time and not contributing to rapport. After the session, the intern divulged what had been worrying her. The co-mediator asked her why she had not just asked the client if she was carrying a gun in her purse. The intern had been too frightened to ask for information directly and really wanted to bolt from the room. She just distanced herself emotionally from the clients. Her unnamed fear produced a pall in the room that made progress impossible. As a result, the mediation ended, relieving the distressed intern but not in a way that was helpful to the client.

In another dramatic situation, a mediator whose partner had committed suicide a year earlier suddenly froze as a client shared concerns about the suicide potential of the other disputant. That mediator, pushed without warning to relive his personal trauma, was flooded with such strong feelings that he could not go forward with the mediation effort and another mediator finished the session. Personal reactions to the people or the content of mediation can be serious blocks to flow.

Another unfortunate and strong block to flow in the mediation room is overidentification with the people, sometimes referred to in therapeutic terms as *counter-transference*. A mediator started a routine session. The client's mannerisms and facial expressions reminded the mediator of his own demanding and unsatisfiable mother. This impression was so strong that it blocked a sense of flow for the mediator, until it bubbled to the surface of his awareness through reflection in action during the session. When the awareness of this impression became conscious, the mediator made a firm decision to keep it to himself and not share it with the disputant, but he also decided not to let this similarity distract him from neutrality, caring, and genuineness during the session. Although there are no guarantees that lack of such external or internal distractions will lead to flow, it is true that for a mediator committed to reflective practice, all impressions are important during interaction, and awareness of these impressions can lead to the flow condition.

For some experienced mediators, the frequency of flow moments seems to diminish rather than flourish. Mediators may become preoccupied with the serious business of making mediation practice economically viable, feeding a family, or building a business. The very things that make talented professionals want to become mediators and to seek artistry in practice seem lost at times. Loss of flow may be symptomatic of a loss of true investment and engagement in the mediation interaction.

Flow gets lost if the mediator loses sight of the goal. Is it to secure written mediated agreements, or to allow disputants a full forum in which to explore their concerns, options, and suggestions? Are mediators functioning so that states and jurisdictions can have diversion programs within the justice system so that the expensive courtroom dockets are not tied up with silly cases that do not deserve a judge's time or attention? Is mediation trying to provide a valuable service because people need help resolving their disputes and society needs more avenues for restorative justice? Are mediators there to meet their own needs or those of their clients? Must these needs be mutually exclusive?

The concept of flow brings into alignment two important demands: meeting the needs of the individuals involved, and meeting society's need for appropriate conflict resolution that gives people more voice and control. When mediators act with artistry and the mediator and the mediation participants experience flow, there is increased likelihood of successful, productive processes taking place in sessions.

Walking the Path of Artistry

Exercise 1: Feeling Flow Outside of Mediation

Establish a routine in your life of doing something creative for ten minutes each day. This could be ten minutes before each session, ten minutes before driving to work, or ten minutes every night before sleeping. It could be playing an instrument, painting or sketching, singing, whittling, shaping clay, or dancing. You can do different mix-and-match activities, or do the activity at different times during the week, but do ten minutes of creative activity each day for one month.

See if you can note when the activity no longer seems like ten minutes but instead seems totally fulfilling and perhaps even absorbs you so much that you have a tendency to continue doing it past the ten-minute limit.

When you realize that has happened, write down your feelings after the activity.

From that point on, do not try to will the experience to come, just recognize it when it does and get in touch with what it does to you. This is the first flush of flow. Enjoy!

Exercise 2: Encouraging Flow During a Session

Remain open to the possibility that flow could occur in the next mediation you do. Assume that it will. Go into your next few sessions with this as a stated aim, then stop thinking about it during the session. Do not let your mind utter the word *flow* until after the session is done. Then critique the session for any of the signs of flow.

- Were there moments when things seemed to be fully absorbing?
- What stopped the flow? What thought, feeling, or impression did you have when it stopped?
- What happened right before the experience?

- Are there things that seemed to trigger it for you? For the disputants? Are these things that you could duplicate, or ephemera that were attached only to those people and that moment?

If you did not experience any flow during the session, ask yourself the following questions:

- Was I feeling scared of anything before or during the session?
- Was I unable to listen with the "third ear" to what the disputants were saying?
- Did some dimension of the disputants' problem resonate for me personally? Is it similar to a personal life experience I have had?

Looking Back, Looking Forward

Flow is not a steady state, a perpetual experience, even for those who are doing the best quality mediation using the principles and methods of reflective practice and interactional process. In a typical mediation session, mediators may experience flow as a periodic occurrence, when all aspects of the interaction are combining synergistically to create this effect. Some have called this a feeling of harmoniousness; some have described it as an easiness that feels unforced and unhurried. Mediators may have this sense of flow, lose it, then regain it as their interventions become more artistic within a session.

Flow is the experience that true artists of all kinds feel when they are acting artistically, with heightened sensitivity to the moment, responding to the subtle changes and interactions between them and the activity they are doing. It requires full engagement and that the full capacity of knowledge and skill be applied in that moment. This flow state is both the goal and the process of artistic mediation practice. When mediators are experiencing flow, they are bringing to bear all the elements of reflective practice, and they can access all their formulations and their constellation of theories in appropriate and extremely skillful ways that contribute to a sense of timelessness. Interactions seem to just happen when a mediator is in flow. Nothing seems forced, uncomfortable, or overly contrived in the interaction.

Flow is the ultimate expression of artistry, the goal of doing reflective practice, the result of a constantly changing interaction. Flow during mediation does not just happen. Mediators must work in the ways that we have described throughout this book to bring the necessary knowledge and skills to bear to create this sense of flow for themselves and their mediation participants. Flow merges process with goal to create the fusion of all elements, the highest expression of the promise of mediation.

In the Conclusion, we will try to bring the realms of reflection and interaction into focus for mediators. If mediators embrace the concepts of artistry, reflection, and interaction, where will these lead us in the practical issues of our time? We will make some recommendations for those who wish to experience more flow and artistry in all stages of their development.

Conclusion

Expanding Artistry in Our Professional Life

This journey ends, but the path continues.

The methods and principles we propose are likely to appear simple, inoffensive, and self-evident. They do not conflict with any model or approach to mediation, and they are based on well-accepted principles of adult education and professional development. Yet their implementation is potentially revolutionary. The implications of the elegant and modest notion that practitioners can attain artistry in practice are profound and far-reaching. Our goal has always been to infuse the field of mediation with a renewed commitment to excellence in practice. We hold the novel and perhaps radical views that mediators have settled for less than their full potential, that artistry is attainable, and that the path to artistry is accessible to all. The methods and principles we describe for making the journey are discernible, proven, and simple to implement.

In this final portion of the book, we summarize the key concepts and examine their implications for education and training, for practice and research. We return to the beginning and explore what we have discovered.

The dynamic four-stage model of professional development describes the path of professional development and helps explain the tasks, skills, and knowledge required to proceed from one stage to the next. Proceeding along the path toward artistry requires that at each stage mediators develop and refine their practice skills and deepen their conceptual knowledge. Additionally, mediators must learn and utilize the principles and practices of reflective practice and interactive process. Knowledge and skill alone are insufficient.

To move forward, mediators must engage in a purposeful, deliberate evaluation of their skills and knowledge through the application of reflective practice and interactive process. The journey from novice to artist is a continuous process of exploration and learning, nurtured by curiosity and the desire for self-improvement. The combination of reflective practice and interactive process will yield artistry.

Here we consider the implications of artistry, reflective practice, and interactive process for the field of mediation, and we examine how the principles and practices we describe might influence the training and education of mediators, the process of coaching, and considerations for certification and credentialing, and we make suggestions for ongoing research. Figure C.1 is a graphic representation that brings together all the mental structures and processes we have described in this book.

When mediators think differently than they do now, they will act differently. We asked ourselves, if mediators and their organizations were following the path to artistry outlined in this book, what would be different? Here are some ideas about how the field of mediation could creatively respond to the concepts and methods we have been developed and described. We want to invite further professional dialogue about these and other ideas that may occur to you, the reader.

Implications for Training and Education

The principles and methods we present in this book are not in conflict with much of the curricula of existing mediation training and educational programs, whether courses of graduate study or the training of new mediators. We do not propose altering the basic pedagogic elements in most of the educational and training programs currently provided. The concepts and methods of reflective practice, interactive process, and artistry are not in conflict with current approaches to mediator training. Introducing them into curricula would enhance the ability of trainees to advance along

Figure C.1. Total Schematic.

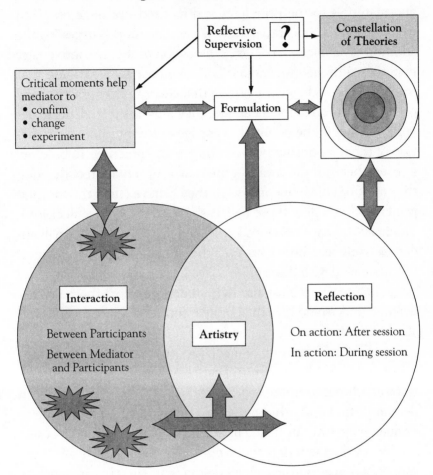

the path of professional development. However, adapting the courses and materials to the principles and methods we have proposed would require a conceptual shift. We are not simply suggesting the addition of scholarly writings or discussion of theories into course materials, although we endorse both approaches. We believe that teachers must embrace the notion that theory guides practice, and on the basis of that understanding they must assist students to develop the discipline required to engage in a continuous examination of the relationship between theory and practice. To be effective, teachers must be aware of their own constellation of theories; they must be able to identify what they believe (their theories and principles) and how those beliefs shape their practice decisions. Teachers who have developed or refined models of practice will understandably teach their students the skills, strategies, and principles associated with those models. We believe, however, that at the same time teachers must also help students explore their own beliefs and understand how their unique constellation of theories will affect their decisions as practitioners.

In the initial training of mediators, we encourage teachers to instill in their students a sense of curiosity. One of the great difficulties with current training approaches is that too often they rely on demonstration and other prescriptive approaches, minimizing or excluding opportunities for a more elicitive approach and focusing on the development of practice responses that mimic those of the trainer. Replication through modeling is an effective approach to teaching skills, but at the same time teachers could nurture students to explore how the students' own beliefs, values, and principles affect their practice. Teaching basic skills is fundamental, especially in the training of novice mediators. Skills are essential elements required for competent practice. But the range of pedagogic methods used must be enlarged. Teachers must nurture curiosity, the springboard to exploration, and encourage students to question, challenge, and investigate, not merely replicate.

At the novice and apprentice stages, mediators are developing their operating systems, the theoretical foundations that ultimately will define their practices. At this early stage in their development, beginning mediators are learning to create and use formulations, to see critical moments during interaction, and to design interventions. We want to sustain the curiosity and enthusiasm that are characteristic of these stages of development and encourage mediators to remain interested in the unknown, uncertain, and surprising opportunities in their practices. At the practitioner level, mediators need to question their interventions and deconstruct their patterns of work in order to understand what premises they are following and whether they need to question those assumptions. All levels of mediators must be encouraged to question, challenge, and investigate, not merely replicate.

If teachers and coaches want to foster the capacity for artistry, they must encourage mediators to be intentional in their work, to reflect in action, to learn continually from their experiences, and to develop the habits and disciplines of reflective practice. Too many mediators practice mindlessly, simply applying the practice skills they were taught in their training programs. They are not focused on the interactional process, and thus are unaware of how their actions affect the participants. When mediators become familiar with and utilize the methods of reflective practice, they will be attuned to the reasons for their interventions as well to as the consequences and risks of those interventions, and they will have the tools to assess their own performance.

The next step in advancing the ideas in this book will be to develop curricular materials to help teachers build reflective practice and interactive process into their courses and programs. We are pleased that at least three university graduate programs (Royal Roads University, Antioch University, and George Mason University) and a mediation certificate program (the Institute for Conflict Analysis and Management in Victoria, British Columbia) have intentionally built their educational programs around the principles and methods of reflective practice. We hope that professional organizations, university curriculum committees, and those who provide mediation training will also look at their curricula and methodology in light of opportunities to nurture the aspiration toward artistry.

Reflective Supervision, Coaching, and Peer Groups

The elicitive coaching method begins with encouraging students to identify and explore their own learning opportunities (critical moments). These choice points in the mediation process are windows into the thinking that leads to action, and by noticing critical moments students understand what is occurring in the interactional process that generates the need for their response. They learn to analyze the events of the mediation with the purpose of becoming aware of their constellation of theories, the beliefs and values that influence how they experience, understand, and make sense of these events. Having such knowledge gives the mediator flexibility, power, and confidence in choosing how to respond to the critical moment.

Through elicitive questions, supervisors and coaches help student mediators illuminate what they are learning (or have learned). This form of coaching nurtures curiosity, encourages exploration, and develops self-reliance. Too much of the coaching we have observed relies on a prescriptive methodology—telling, instructing, correcting, criticizing, and evaluating. This approach tends to produce conformity. Although there are virtues in the prescriptive approach, we are deeply concerned that students are learning a model without understanding the underlying principles and beliefs. Although there is a place for the prescriptive approach, we have learned that an elicitive methodology encourages exploration, self-discovery, and creation. The use of elicitive questions values students' knowledge and fosters learning in areas that are most useful. The mind-set of the elicitive teacher is that of a facilitator, a guide, one who provides opportunities for the student to experiment and learn.

Reflective coaching leads to artistry. Guiding students to identify their strengths and weaknesses, as well as areas of uncertainty and awkwardness, helps them learn to explore the questions and dilemmas presented by critical moments. Through their reflection and analysis, they learn to develop unique responses to the surprising events of practice.

Unfortunately, many practitioners do not have good opportunities for reflective coaching. Mediators often function as sole proprietors, or in busy community or court agencies where they scarcely have time to debrief the case and write a few notes into the file before they are off to the next set of clients. Finding and making the time for reflective coaching, as well as having the opportunity to receive it, can be problematic.

If the concepts presented in this book have been instructive and practitioners want this level of coaching, they may need to build new structures. For example, the coaching methods we describe work quite well with peer consultation models, in which practitioners help one another to develop the practices and learn the principles of reflective practice. Peer consultation models do not generally rely on a leader, thus allowing diversity and creativity. The use of peer consultation models built around the reflective practice methods and concepts will certainly enhance the potential for mediators to attain artistry in their practices.

The professional organizations in our field should take an increased role in stimulating interest in professional development. Current approaches, such as encouraging continuing education, requiring supervision as a condition of membership, and setting standards for training programs are important contributions. Without a commitment to lifelong learning, however, these efforts, no matter how well intended and carefully implemented, are unlikely to produce an artistic level of professional development. In most other professions, newly educated practitioners have the benefit of mentors, experienced professionals who help the novice gain proficiency, capacity, and competence. Only the Academy of Family Mediators, as a requirement for advanced membership status, requires candidates to complete a minimum number of hours of supervision. The process for mentoring is inadequate, yet it remains the single example of organizationally supported mentoring in the field.

We encourage leaders in the field of mediation—those who set the policies, standards, and criteria—to implement the practices and approaches we describe in this book. Responding to this challenge would require the organizations to develop and implement educational programs that nurture curiosity, exploration, innovation, and discovery. These programs would not be concerned so much with the model of practice as with the quality of practice. They would help articulate and support the implementation of peer supervision models and other methods of assisting mediators to attain proficiency. In this regard, we applaud the efforts of Family Mediation Canada to design and implement a mediator certification program that inspires mediators to further their skills and knowledge.

Of those who have a deep interest in professional development, we ask, If your curricula reflected the principles and methods that nurture artistry, what would be different and what would you retain? Is it possible to design a training program or academic course that enhances the capacity for professional achievement? We encourage both the training of mediators in the essential skills and principles of practice, and the nurturing of their professional development toward artistry.

Certification, Competency, and Credentialing

A number of professional organizations, including the Academy of Family Mediators and Family Mediation Canada, have embarked on efforts to identify the practice techniques and knowledge required of a skillful, effective mediator as a basis for creating a testing or assessment process to determine competency. We are concerned that the result of these efforts may be the establishment of standards that do not adequately address the variety of models, approaches, and methods used by mediators, and that by setting criteria these groups may ultimately establish more of a ceiling than a floor in terms of professional competence.

Family Mediation Canada is working to address these twin concerns by developing and implementing an assessment process that is developmental, that does not simply grade or judge a mediator's ability to meet certain professional standards, but nourishes the aspiration toward excellence. Their process, using either live or videotaped mediation sessions, engages the applicants in a dialogue with the assessors. The purpose of the dialogue is to identify the critical moments in the mediation, to inquire how the mediator experienced and responded to those events, to identify the choice of interventions, and to explore the mediator's reasons for those choices.

Another feature of this assessment process is the explicit notion that the assessors will talk with candidates who do not meet the criteria and will help them identify the problem areas and the issues they must address in order to receive approval. The assessors view themselves not as judges but as coaches; they assist and guide the candidates toward eventual certification. The goal of the program is for every candidate to develop the skills and knowledge necessary for certification.

We believe that credentialing or certification efforts should adopt the values that underlie the model used in Canada. The approach should be aspirational, not prescriptive; it should encourage learning, creativity, and professional development, not the attainment of a particular set of standards. A process that supports inventiveness, continued learning, and movement toward artistry will serve the field well.

Currently in the United States, some states, such as Florida, have established standards for mediators in certain types of disputes. Family and civil disputes, for example, require mediators to have completed an approved training program as well as to have a graduate degree. Once the mediators meet these criteria, there is no ongoing effort to assess their competency and to encourage their continued learning. Mediators are not required to participate in supervision or coaching sessions, and there is no formal or informal

mentoring process, nor any other feedback loop by which mediators can reflect on their mediation experiences. Although some
jurisdictions require continuing education, these training programs
do not as a rule provide the type of learning opportunity that is
essential to the development of artistry in practice.

According to recent research by Maureen E. Lauflin (1999) at
the University of Idaho, nine or more states currently require that
civil mediators be licensed attorneys in order to practice mediation;
in addition, eight states, plus the province of Ontario, require that
civil mediators have knowledge of legal processes. Although we do
not dispute the value of such professional education or substantive
information, we are concerned that law degrees and legal information alone do not provide practitioners with the ability to practice artistically. To achieve this measure of excellence in practice
requires a grounding in theory, the application of the reflective
practice approach, and attention to the interactional process.
These concepts are ideas to which all practitioners, despite their
profession of origin, can ascribe. In states where the only criterion
for mediation is a law degree, the path toward artistry will serve as
a hedge against this regulatory approach based on a single factor.
We have met many practitioners from legal backgrounds who were
very conversant with and practiced the concepts in this book. Following the path of artistry we have laid out may be a way to bridge
the widening gap between those who have legal training and those
who do not, and thereby reduce the growing schism within the
field. Designating one official background or degree for this work
will not ensure quality practice and may simply create destructive
and unnecessary divisions among mediators.

Artistry is attainable by anyone who actively travels the path.
It is not dependent on a particular degree or license. If practicing
mediators, from whatever professional background, were to acknowledge that the path to artistry is a lifelong process of learning,
they would insist on measures of competency other than a mediator's professional license or academic training. They would want to

encourage the creativity, exploration, and innovation characteristic of artistic practice.

Research and Development

We encourage researchers to question, challenge, and investigate the assumptions, values, and methods we propose and their conceptual foundations. For example, our teaching and coaching rely heavily on an elicitive method. Does this approach achieve the goals we propose? What method will most likely assist mediators to develop the capacities that lead to artistry? Does recognition of critical moments contribute to the outcome of mediation efforts? We also invite research into the four-stage model we have created. Is this a realistic, accurate, and useful representation of the path of professional development? We see so many questions that could be researched to provide support for or refine these ideas, yet at present there are few if any organized research endeavors investigating the phenomena and practices that we believe contribute to artistic practice.

Our notions of artistry and of the path of professional development are not connected to any particular form of practice, to any one model. In recent years a growing debate about the transformative and problem-solving approaches has gained considerable attention, as has the discussion stimulated by efforts to distinguish between facilitative and evaluative styles. But the principles and practices we have developed and described in this book are universal; they are not limited to any one form of practice.

We have successfully taught these ideas and practices to those who steadfastly hold to their belief in a model of practice that depends on evaluation, direction, and problem solving. Mediators who adhere to principles of empowerment and recognition have also found these concepts and practices to be highly effective in achieving excellence in their work. We believe that the concepts and methods of reflective practice and attention to the dynamic interactional process transcend the dichotomies of attorney-mediator versus mental-health-based mediator, or problem-solving versus transformative approaches. When mediators are acting out of the concepts we have outlined, they can hold radically different beliefs and enact very different models of practice yet practice with artistry. Our concepts are a way to bridge the diversity in the field and unify it while still allowing these creative differences.

End of the Journey: Following the Path

Artistry transcends any boundaries of practice models, has universal applicability, and is the key to professional satisfaction and competence. Nurturing the aspiration toward artistry is our goal. We believe in the potential of each individual to seek and attain professional excellence. We also believe that reflective practice and interactive process will, if applied with intention and commitment, yield artistry. We invite you to begin or continue your journey.

References

Argyris, C., and Schön, D. A. *Theory in Practice: Increasing Professional Effectiveness*. San Francisco: Jossey-Bass, 1974.

Boulding, K. *Three Faces of Power*. Thousand Oaks, Calif.: Sage, 1989.

Bush, R.A.B., and Folger, J. P. *The Promise of Mediation: Responding to Conflict Through Empowerment and Recognition*. San Francisco: Jossey-Bass, 1994.

Csikszentmihalyi, M. *Flow: The Psychology of Optimal Experience*. New York: HarperCollins, 1991.

Csikszentmihalyi, M. *The Evolving Self: A Psychology for the Third Millennium*. New York: HarperCollins, 1993.

Csikszentmihalyi, M. *Creativity: Flow and the Psychology of Discovery and Invention*. New York: HarperCollins, 1996.

Csikszentmihalyi, M. *Finding Flow: The Psychology of Engagement with Everyday Life*. New York: Basic Books, 1997.

Feer, M. "On Toward a New Discourse for Mediation: A Critique of Neutrality." *Mediation Quarterly*, 1992, 10(2), 173–177.

Fisher, R., and Ury, W. *Getting to Yes*. New York: Penguin, 1983. (Originally published 1981.)

Folberg, J., and Taylor, A. *Mediation*. San Francisco: Jossey-Bass, 1984.

Folger, J., Poole, M., and Stutman, R. *Working Through Conflict*. (3rd ed.) Reading, Mass.: Addison-Wesley, 1997.

Galbraith, J. K. "Power and Organization." In S. Lukes (ed.), *Power*. New York: New York University Press, 1986. (Originally published 1983 [1984])

Galtung, J. *Peace by Peaceful Means: Peace and Conflict, Development and Civilization*. Sage (Prio), 1996.

Gibran, K. *The Prophet*. New York: Knopf, 1995.

Goleman, D., Kaufman, P., and Ray, M. *The Creative Spirit*. New York: Penguin Books, 1993.

Gottman, J. *What Predicts Divorce? The Relationship Between Marital Processes and Marital Outcomes*. Hillsdale, N.J.: Erlbaum, 1993.

Haynes, J. "Power Balancing." In J. Folberg (ed.), *Divorce Mediation: Theory and Practice*. New York: Guilford Press, 1989.

Irving, H., and Benjamin, M. *Family Mediation: Contemporary Issues*. Thousand Oaks, Calif.: Sage, 1995.

Johnston, J., and Roseby, V. *In the Name of the Child: A Developmental Approach to Understanding and Helping Children of Conflicted and Violent Divorce*. New York: Free Press, 1997.

Kosko, B. *Fuzzy Thinking: The New Science of Fuzzy Logic*. New York: Hyperion, 1993.

Kriesberg, L. *Constructive Conflicts: From Escalation to Resolution*. Lanham. Md.: Rowman and Littlefield, 1998.

Langer, E. J. *Mindfulness*. Reading, Mass.: Addison-Wesley, 1989.

Langer, E. J. *The Power of Mindful Learning*. Reading, Mass.: Addison-Wesley, 1997.

Lauflin, M. E. Handout. Eighth Annual Northwest ADR Conference, April 1999.

Lederach, J. P. *Preparing for Peace: Conflict Transformation Across Cultures*. Syracuse, New York: Syracuse University Press, 1995.

Moore, C. *The Mediation Process*. (2nd ed.) San Francisco: Jossey-Bass, 1996.

Piercy, F., and Nelson, T. "Flow in the Consultation Room." *The Family Therapy Networker*, Jan./Feb. 1999, 46–47.

Rifkin, J., Millen, J., and Cobb, S. "Toward a New Discourse for Mediation: A Critique of Neutrality." *Mediation Quarterly*, 1991, 9(2), 151–164.

Riskin, L. "Understanding Mediator Orientations, Strategies, and Techniques: A Grid for the Perplexed." *Harvard Law Review*, 1996, 7, 7–51.

Rummel, R. J. *The Conflict Helix: The Principles and Practices of Interpersonal, Social, and International Conflict and Cooperation*. New Brunswick, N.J.: Transaction Publishers, 1991. (Originally published in 1984 as *In the Minds of Men*. Seoul, Korea: Sogang University Press.)

Russell, B. In S. Lukes (ed.), *Power*. New York: New York University Press, 1986. (Originally published 1938.)

Satir, V. *Peoplemaking*. Palo Alto, Calif.: Science and Behavior Books, 1972.

Schön, D. A. *The Reflective Practitioner: How Professionals Think in Action*. New York: Basic Books, 1983.

Schön, D. A. *Educating the Reflective Practitioner: Toward a New Design for Teaching and Learning in the Professions*. San Francisco: Jossey-Bass, 1987.

Simmel, G. "Domination and Freedom." In S. Lukes (ed.), *Power*. New York: New York University Press, 1986. (Originally published 1950.)

Sowell, T. *A Conflict of Visions: Ideological Origins of Political Struggles*. New York: William Morrow, 1987.

Taylor, A. "Concepts of Neutrality in Family Mediation: Contexts, Ethics, Influence, and Transformative Process." *Mediation Quarterly*, 1997, 14(3), 215–236.

Weber, M. "Domination by Economic Power and Authority." In S. Lukes (ed.),

Power. New York: New York University Press, 1986. (Originally published 1978.)

Wheatley, M. J. *Leadership and the New Science: Learning About Organization from an Orderly Universe.* San Francisco: Berrett-Koehler, 1993.

Wilmot, W. W., and Hocker, J. L. *Interpersonal Conflict.* (5th ed.) Boston: McGraw Hill, 1998.

Additional Resources

Becoming a Reflective Practitioner

Argyris, C., and Schön, D. A. *Theory in Practice: Increasing Professional Effectiveness*. San Francisco: Jossey-Bass Publishers, 1974.

Benjamin, R. D. "The Physics of Mediation: Reflections of Scientific Theory in Professional Practice." *Mediation Quarterly*, Volume 8, Number 2, 1990.

Birkhoff, J. E., and Warfield, W. "The Development of Pedagogy and Practicum." *Mediation Quarterly*, Volume 14, Number 2, 1997.

Burton, J. *Conflict Resolution as a Political System*, Working Paper No. 1. Fairfax, VA: Center for Conflict Analysis and Resolution, George Mason University, 1988.

Bush, R.A.B., and Folger, J. P. *The Promise of Mediation*. San Francisco: Jossey-Bass Publishers, 1995.

Csikszentmihalyi, M. *Creativity: Flow and the Psychology of Discovery and Invention*. New York: HarperCollins Publishers, 1996.

Friere, P. *Pedagogy of the Oppressed*. New York: The Continuum Publishing Company, 1993.

Gulliver, P. H.. *Disputes and Negotiation: A Cross-Cultural Perspective*. Orlando, FL: Academic Press, 1979.

Kritek, P. B. *Negotiating at an Uneven Table: Developing Moral Courage in Resolving Our Conflicts*. San Francisco: Jossey-Bass Publishers, 1994.

Langer, E. J. *Mindfulness*. Reading, MA: Addison Wesley Publishing Company, 1989.

Langer, E. J. *The Power of Mindful Learning*. Reading, MA: Addison Wesley Publishing Company, 1997.

Schein, E. *Professional Education*. New York: McGraw-Hill, 1973.

Schön, D. A. *The Reflective Practitioner*. San Francisco: Jossey-Bass Publishers, 1987.

Schön, D. A. *Educating The Reflective Practitioner: How Professionals Think in Action*. New York: Basic Books, 1983.

Senge, P. M. *The Fifth Discipline: The Art and Practice of the Learning Organization*. New York: Currency-Doubleday, 1990.

Wheatley, M. J. *Leadership and the New Science: Learning about Organization from an Orderly Universe*. San Francisco: Berrett-Koehler Publishers, Inc., 1993.

Unifying Theories and Definitional Bases

Folger, J. P., Poole, M. S., and Stutman, R. K. *Working Through Conflict*, 3rd Edition. New York: Addison Wesley Longman, 1997.

Galtung, J. *Peace by Peaceful Means: Peace and Conflict, Development and Civilization*. London: Sage Publications, 1996.

Kreisberg, L. *Constructive Conflicts: From Escalation to Resolution*. Lanham, MD: Rowman & Littlefield, 1998.

Rummel, R. J. *The Conflict Helix: Principles & Practices of Interpersonal, Social and International Conflict and Cooperation*. New Brunswick, NJ: Transaction Publishers, 1991.

Schellenberg, J. A. *Conflict Resolution: Theory, Research, and Practice*. New York: SUNY, 1996.

Background Understandings

Augsburger, D. *Conflict Mediation Across Cultures: Pathways and Patterns*. Louisville, KY: Westminster/John Knox Press, 1992.

Boulding, K. *Three Faces of Power*. Newbury Park, CA: Sage Publications, 1990 (1989).

Bunker, B., and Rubin, J., (eds.). *Conflict, Cooperation and Justice: Essays Inspired by the Work of Morton Deutsch*. San Francisco: Jossey-Bass, 1995.

Coates, R. B., Kalanj, B., and Umbreit, M. S. *Victim Meets Offender: The Impact of Restorative Justice and Mediation*. Monsey, NY: Willow Tree Press, 1994.

Feagin, J. R. *Social Problems: A Critical Power—Conflict Perspective*, 5th Ed. Englewood Cliffs, NJ: Prentice-Hall, 1996.

Felson, R. B., and Tedeschi, J. T. (eds.). *Aggression & Violence: Social Interactionist Perspectives*. American Psychological Association, 1993.

Galaway, B., and Hudson, J., (eds.). *Restorative Justice: International Perspectives*. Monsey, NY: Willow Tree Press, 1996.

Lukes, S. (ed.). *Power*. Washington Square, NY: New York University Press, 1986.

O'Connor, J., and McDermott, I. *The Art of Systems Thinking: Essential Skills for Creativity and Problem Solving*. London: Thorsons (Harper Collins), 1997.

Rothman, J. *Resolving Identity-Based Conflicts*. San Francisco: Jossey-Bass, 1997.

Sowell, T. *A Conflict of Visions: Ideological Origins of Political Struggles*. New York: William Morrow, 1987.

Models of Mediation and Negotiation

Bush, R.A.B., and Folger, J. P. *The Promise of Mediation: Responding to Conflict Through Empowerment and Recognition*. San Francisco: Jossey-Bass, 1994.

Irving, H., and Benjamin, M. *Family Mediation: Contemporary Issues*. Thousand Oaks, CA: Sage, 1995.

Lewicki, R., Saunder, D., and Minton, J. *Essentials of Negotiation*. Chicago: Erwin, 1997.

Moore, C. *The Mediation Process*, 2nd Ed. San Francisco: Jossey-Bass, 1996.

Slaikeu, K. A. *When Push Comes to Shove: A Practical Guide to Mediating Disputes*. San Francisco: Jossey-Bass, 1996.

Understanding Family Dynamics

Johnston, J. and Roseby, V. *In the Name of the Child*. New York: Free Press, 1997.

Walsh, F. (Ed.). *Normal Family Processes*, 2nd Ed. New York: Guilford, 1993.

Index